The Unity Way

By
Marcus Bach

UNITY BOOKS
Unity Village, MO 64065

Second Edition 1986

Cover photograph by
Keith McKinney

Contents

Before We Begin   Of Books and Immortality

Part One: Profiles of the Past
(1940s—1960s)

Part Two: Patterns for the Present
(1960s—1980s)

Part Three: Perspective on the Future
(1980s—21st Century)

Before We Begin

Of Books and Immortality

Books are often referred to as "brain children," and rightly so. Not unlike the children of one's flesh and blood, these creative siblings, born by choice or chance, are destined to have lives of their own. Their experiences in the world compare favorably to those of any other seminal offspring. All of the human emotions are theirs, and no doubt their secret fear is that they may someday be permanently shelved and forgotten.

Whoever fathers or mothers these literary progeny often fails to realize that, though these published wordlings may remain young at heart in their parent's eyes, they nonetheless grow up and reach an age of accountability, just like the rest of us.

This, in effect, is what has happened to a brain child of mine who was born under the Prentice-Hall imprint in 1962 and was appropriately christened "The Unity Way of Life," later published by Unity Books under the same title.

It was a most legitimate and adventurous

child, self-willed and sensitive. As a doting father, I cannot resist pointing out that it was the seventh in a prolific family which has now grown to twenty-five. This seventh member, *The Unity Way of Life,* still circulates widely, enjoys a worldwide readership, has been honored in six editions, appeared in a variety of jackets, been hosted by book clubs, and has lured many questing souls into the Unity fellowship. But it reached a maturity somewhat beyond its years and, in the language of the trade, is now definitely out of print.

All of this raised the inevitable question which, I feel, the out-of-print book itself is asking, "Where do I go from here? Since I was born in the sixties, what do people think of me now in the 1980s? And where will I be in another twenty years?"

In fact, the book often said to me point-blank, "Tell me, sir, are you, as a good parent, planning to speak through me again, or what do you have in mind? Have you ever thought of letting me speak for myself?"

I gathered from this that its concern was not so much a matter of survival as of continuity. And that is why, when editor Thomas Witherspoon and officials at Unity headquarters proposed an updating or a new version of *The Unity Way of Life,* I was quite prepared in my decision. I suggested that this metaphysically-oriented seventh child might conceivably consent to a literary reincarnation into a brain child of today in which the same indomitable soul "with strengthened limb and quickened brain, would once more walk the road again."

The plan was considered well worth a try, and now that it is prepared to start its journey and have its say, we christened it *The Unity Way,* knowing full well that it will nostalgically reflect Unity's yesterday, Unity's today, and a venture into Unity's tomorrow—when the century turns.

Marcus Bach

Part One

Profiles of the Past

(1940s—1960s)

Chapter I

Divine Order
(Charles and Myrtle Fillmore)

Certain places and people play recurring roles in one's life. By a strange mix of circumstances the unexpected often happens as if it had been deliberately planned. Call it fate, luck, karma, or simply serendipity, some events seem foreordained, the result of an immutable law of cause and effect, balanced on the razor's edge of chance.

One of the places intricately interwoven into my early life was Kansas City, Missouri, and one of the people was Charles Fillmore, cofounder of a now worldwide spiritual fellowship, Unity School of Christianity.

Long ago, longer than I care to admit, I was called to serve as minister of an Evangelical church in Kansas City on the corner of 36th and Wabash. I was a fledgling preacher, newly ordained in the German Reformed denomination, enthusiastic, and eager to save the world before everybody became so religious they wouldn't need saving.

Kansas City was my challenge and I accepted the charge. The church was a lovely, intimate house of worship built of quarried stone, partially vine-covered, with a belfry and a bell. Whenever I pulled the bell-rope on a Sunday morning, I recalled how my bearded preacher-uncle used to let me ring the bell in my hometown church when I was a child in a little Wisconsin town. He always stood nearby, keeping God's eye on me, annoyed that on the final hefty pull I would let the rope lift me off my feet as if I were being borne aloft, up to where the ringing is.

Now I had my own church and my own bell and 280 parishioners who were already saved. So I talked mostly about the oneness of all religions and interdenominational mergers, and the like, without realizing that I was letting the rope pull me higher than I was supposed to go.

I stayed on for an ambitious year and a half before concluding that I had misread my calling. My interest was definitely more centered in a curiosity about what others believed and why they believed it than in converting anyone to a single sectarian expression. Secretly, the term "denomination" always seemed to me to represent merely one small arc in the total circumference of religious faith.

Though my parishioners truly loved me

and I loved them, they were not ready for a fellowship of all faiths. What they wanted in those days was faith in our particular fellowship. I told them later, as we kept in touch through the years, that I had been a hero among them twice, the day I came and the day I left.

The timing wasn't right.

Or was it?

But for that pastorate I might never have seen life and religion in a perspective that became for me the outworking of something more than fate or chance. It became a career in religious research which was to evolve into a lifework, and but for the place, Kansas City, I might never have met the person, Charles Fillmore.

His influence was to move in and out of my life as it has in the lives of countless others, most of whom were deprived of meeting him in person or catching the impact of his physical presence. But that may be neither here nor there. We all have our destinies. We all create our own philosophies, and eventually we all forge our own beliefs.

We all know that we live in a most uncertain world if we have nothing more to believe in than chance. And we eventually learn that, in the history of events, as in the history of

3

every life, there is a chain of cause and effect, and in some transfigured moment we realize that things are always rightly put together on a new plane of spiritual understanding.

Mystics have referred to this phenomenon as the spiritual synthesis of our thoughts, words, and deeds. Many have speculated that reincarnation plays a role in it. Psychoanalysts have called it synchronicity. Others use the terms centroversion, the Omega Point, the fullness of time. Unity calls it divine order.

And well it might, for the history of Unity's first fifty years, since its inception in 1889, is the history of events in the lives of two particular people: Charles and Myrtle Fillmore. Rarely in the records of contemporary religions do we find the evidence and meaning of divine order charted as clearly as in a profile of Unity's past. It is here that we find a first clue to Unity's success: People who instinctively identified with the Fillmores in their quest recognized a new, adventurous self-discovery in the teachings that became the Unity way, and a new religion was launched in the mainstream of American life.

I first met Charles Fillmore in 1942 at Unity's headquarters, 917 Tracy Avenue, in Kansas City. It was a rainy autumn morning, but the smallish, energetic man had utter disregard for the weather. He was bareheaded, exhilarated, it seemed to me, by the touch of the rain in his wisps of thin, white hair, and thrilled at the fact that his hands were opening the copper-grilled door to what might have been some celestial hideaway.

His face was strong but gentle. Deep-set blue eyes and the confident hint of a smile had a way of saying that all was well with the world because all was well with him. His manner was that of a young man who had run through the rain catching the drops in his mouth, flushed with a sense of nature's friendly response. His ears were large, a fact I recalled particularly because of my impression that he did not really need them at all. As he sat at his rolltop desk and I on a cushioned kitchen chair in his modest office, his art of listening, as far as I was concerned, was psychic, as if interpreting the spirit of my questions rather than the spoken word.

Had you been with me as we entered his office you might not have noticed that he limped slightly, and it would have stretched your credulity to believe that for twenty years and more he walked with the aid of a brace. A boyhood skating accident left him with a deteriorated hip. A doctor's prognosis warned him that he was destined to drag his "withered leg" for the rest of his life. Yet, catching his vibrations of some hidden mystical insight, you would have reflected seriously on his testimony that by spiritual power, mind power, God power, call it what you will, he graduated from braces to crutches to a cane and then to running unaided through an autumn rain. You might have asked yourself, as I did, about the depth of faith and the prayer experiences in our lives from childhood on. You might have shared my thoughts, "He represents something *other worldly* that tantalizes me. There is a wistfully disarming quality about him that hints of a secret discovery I, too, have felt."

There was no consciousness of age about Charles Fillmore, but I had been told that he was eighty-eight.

What intrigued me during this meeting with "Papa Charley," as many of his followers affectionately called him, was my off-and-on impression that this real-estate-man-turned-religionist had learned some constructive, practical truths in the seminary of life that were not included in the theological school where I was trained for the traditional ministry. More than a quarter of a century earlier he had phased out a successful real estate business because he had a call, not from a church, but from a Presence within himself.

Somehow, somewhere, Fillmore learned to put God and man together in a cooperative adventure, ending a spiritual standoff that had long existed in the teachings of the institutionalized churches. There was an intimacy in Unity that closed the gap, not only between God and the individual, but between heaven and earth and most of all, between universal mind and human mind, as though there were indeed just one mind, God's Mind.

This was different from the philosophy with which I had been indoctrinated. I shared with him a corny illustration often used in sermonizing. The one about the minister who, complimenting a farmer on his abundant acres, said, "God and you have done an excellent job here." To which the farmer replied, "Guess we did. You should have seen it when God had the place all by Himself."

Papa Charley chuckled politely at this old joke, but it did not suit him. God never had anything by Himself. Neither did man. It was a cosmic caretakership from the beginning. His theory was that the many who live in the One represent the One who lives in the many.

But he had a sense of humor and said I should wait and see what God had done with the acres of land out at Unity Farm which had stood idle for several years, but to which the Unity headquarters was currently being moved, and which would be its permanent home, seventeen miles southeast of Kansas City near Lee's Summit. Had I ever been there?

"By chance" I had. I explained that during my pastorate at 36th and Wabash a parishioner of mine, concerned about my interest in the new "cults" that were coming along, took me out to show me what he called "Fillmore's Folly." There were several buildings and a campanile out there in those days, a grown-over golf course, and a sort-of-lake. There were no adjoining highways, nothing to indicate that these undulating brush-covered fields and neglected meadows would ever come to life. Our car bogged down in the mud that day not far from an unimposing sign that said, *Unity Farm.* Prophetically my friend proclaimed that the "cult called Unity" would remain equally bogged down and decidedly short-lived.

Papa Charley laughed lightly as I told him the story. He said he would arrange for his son Rick to take me over the grounds, a fifty-acre tract of farm and woodland that had been purchased in 1920. Building projects were almost immediately begun in the prosperous twenties. A Silent Unity sanctuary was constructed to serve as a prayer and healing center. The entire site was designed as a rest and recreation area, a place for spiritual renewing, an energizing center for learning and applying Truth principles. The grounds had been blessed. Charles and Myrtle Fillmore had proclaimed them, "A bit of heaven on Earth." Then came the depression. The work had to be abandoned. The Unity workers moved back to Tracy Avenue.

Now, some twenty years later, divine order had established its proper timing. Fillmore had not the slightest question about that. No doubt, no anxiety, no concern. He rested with enviable ease in his faith. In this light, the concept of what is commonly called chance, fate, or fortune took on the recognition that God and self and events converge in convincing demonstrations of what God-power and the God-spell are all about. His words were fired with high adventure and a youthful passion as he told me about Unity's adventure and its prospects for days ahead. America was beginning to respond to the Unity way of life.

Somehow it did not seem incongruous to me just then that in this little room on Tracy an ordinary, self-educated man with extraordinary convictions should draw both wisdom and vision from an infinite, cosmic Source and make them practical as usable techniques for human achievement.

The profile of Unity's past as seen in Charles Fillmore was not only the story of a spiritual movement but a lesson in truth of the movement of Spirit in every individual who explores the deeper reach of life. The same experiences, from challenges to eventual awareness of divine order, are, in short, reflexive, and by way of those who have experienced them, we discover the path of unfoldment within ourselves.

He spoke of the story of Unity—its birth, its growth, its teachings—almost shyly, as if feeling me out on both my interest in these matters and my ability to comprehend them. We felt a oneness. And during our visit, I recall, he never lost the confident smile, the hint that there was always something profoundly more beneath the surface than simple words could tell.

Charles Fillmore's birth and boyhood, God knows, were humble enough. He was born in a log cabin near St. Cloud, Minnesota, on the morning of August 22, 1854, on the edge of a Chippewa Indian reservation. His birth sign was Leo, on the cusp of Virgo.

When during his youth his parents separated, he assumed responsibility for supporting his mother and a younger brother. His relationship with Mother Fillmore was to become part of the Unity story, and the loyalties between them ran deeply through the consciousness of all that Charles was to represent in the way of love and family relations.

Throughout a tough, hardworking adulthood and, at times, a roving adventurousness in an America as restless as himself, he was driven by an insatiable quest for a practical philosophy to live by. Self-educated, influenced by the writings of the greatest transcendentalist and creative thinker of the time, Ralph Waldo Emerson, he may or may not have known that the spiritual die was cast.

"I literally lived with Emerson," he told me in speaking of the renowned Sage of Concord. And through the writings of other contemporary luminaries—Alcott, Lowell, Thoreau, Mark Twain—he also lived with them, at least vicariously. He read practically everything they wrote.

Unity was one day to talk and teach about

"divine guidance." Charles Fillmore was being inescapably trained in the course during these formative years. Working at odd jobs—store clerk, printer's devil, clerical positions—he was driven by an inner urge for the kind of self-fulfillment we all feel and find, if we will, somewhere along the way. Inspired by the Bible, sensitized by the genius of Tennyson, Shakespeare, and Wordsworth, touching the creative flow of universal Mind, he turned to the religious movements of his day to discover on his own what was true or false. It was Fillmore in development and Unity in the making.

The mid-19th century was one of the most innovative and iconoclastic epochs in America's history. The established churches were caught in a crosscurrent of apocalyptic frenzy. Adventists were picking up the pieces of their predictions that the end of the world had come and gone. The Mormon trek was a dramatic demonstration of the indomitable fervor of the Latter Day Saints. Spiritualism, old as the Scriptures but born anew in America in 1848, had now become a religion. Pentecostalism and other fundamentalists were speaking of a "Great Awakening," an upcoming revival mightier than the "Upper Room." Utopian groups and mutualistic movements—the Amanas, Anaheim, the Perfectionists, Icaria, the Harmony Society—were establishing their communes.

Protestantism and Catholicism were shoring up against these trends while bracing themselves against a more formidable "foe": the "anti-Christian" phalanxes of Christian Science and "New Thought Truth Work" linked to a heresy called "metaphysics." The term itself was a shocker to the church-at-large. Some said it was linked to Aristotle who lived 500 years before the time of Jesus Christ. Church scholars traced metaphysics to theosophy and the occult. Evangelists denounced it as originating from a mesmerist, Phineas Parkhurst Quimby, promoted by Mary Baker Eddy, spawned by Emersonian "free thinkers," another name for agnostics or atheists and anti-Christs. Prelates made short shrift of New Thought generally, by branding it as a heresy.

In such a torrent, where was a still unclassified searching soul such as Charles Fillmore to go? He took a good, hard look at institutionalized religions and turned away from their closed doors and preconceived dogmatic minds. He investigated spiritualism and found it interesting and inconclusive. Impressed by concepts of "eternalism" for a time, he believed that the body had the capacity to continually restore itself with a new "cellular structure" every seven years, and that if a person learned nature's secrets it might be possible to vanquish death.

He became an eclectic, a synthesizer of what he felt was Truth, and the impact of this on Unity's teaching would one day be crystal clear. He believed in reincarnation as a theory worthy of consideration, and this, too, was to influence the Unity movement. His openness to so-called seers and prophets, and his investigative mind, gave proof of his own vision of living free in the adventurous field of the quest. And always there was Emerson. Emerson the man, the philosopher, the pragmatist, idealist, who was one day to be called, rightly or not, the father of New Thought. And there was Emerson's intuitive feeling about God as being Omnipotent, Omniscient, Omnipresent—God as universal Mind and Spirit, teaching the unity of individual life and unity with nature's laws so that in the words of New Thought thinking: "In the exaltation of our own spirit we can say with the master Teacher: *'I and the Father are one!'* " (John 10:30).

It must have been this period that Papa Charley had in mind when he said to me,

"Life is a spiral climb with no other way to go than up!" And it was during the metamorphosis of his life and America's history in the decades of the mid-1880s that he intensified his climb. And as I think of it, I realize he was belabored not only with the ordinary confrontations that often beset us all but with something more. He was dragging not only his "withered leg" but the deeply indoctrinated medical warning that he would never walk normally again.

Obviously, the doctors had not taken God into account as Charles Fillmore decided to do at this particular point in human time. Why should they have thought of God? Are there case histories in medical annals reporting that a withered leg can be restored through prayer and discipline and affirmations? The Great Physician was not listed in biographies of medical practitioners. The Scriptures said He healed the sick and raised the dead but rarely, if ever, were His cases discussed in professional medical circles. He stood a lonely, solitary figure, believed in, worshiped, tolerated, doubted, and frequently rejected. Fillmore turned to God through Christ, or through the Christ to God, and someday Unity would seek to make things clear.

There is always a tendency to romanticize those whose faith has made them whole. Endless legends surround both healers and the healed who have demonstrated in actuality what they proclaimed in some great mountaintop experience. The withered leg made whole in Fillmore's case is not a legend but a learning.

And if I read the story correctly, even Charles Fillmore would not—or might not—have been healed, and the Unity movement might never have been born had it not been that, through a spectacular series of sequences, spun by the stars of choice or chance, a second player was introduced into the Fillmore drama: Myrtle Page of Pagetown, Ohio, cast in the role of Charles' wife. And not as a wife only, but as a way-shower and questmate for more than half a century. It simply would not have happened unless, of course, you have by now begun to believe in a basic Unity idea: divine order.

From the day of their marriage in 1881, this husband-wife partnership was built on deeply personal needs and aspirations. The Unity movement, even before it had a name, was not founded but cofounded. We are talking now about the genesis of Unity, its "ancient history," the mid-1880s and early 1890s, before the word "Unity" was revealed to Charles in a moment of reverie. We are thinking now of how mysteriously God moves in other lives so that we, in turn, will better understand His working in our own.

For, all the while that Charles was seeking Truth and guidance in his world, Myrtle Page had been on a similar path in a world of her own. The differences in these worlds were striking, the likenesses phenomenal.

Myrtle was born August 6, 1845, under the sign of Leo, as was Charles. Her birthplace, Pagetown, Ohio, named in honor of her father, Marcus Page, was a sparsely settled farming community located near Walnut Creek in Morrow County. The eighth child in a family of nine, Myrtle grew up in the tradition of Methodism which had a meeting house in an adjoining neighborhood. It would be fair to say, in the idiom of the time, that Marcus Page was a pillar of the church and apparently held sternly to the Wesleyan discipline that included "a desire to flee from the wrath to come and to be saved from your sins." He championed a God of righteousness. Lucy, Myrtle's mother, was also a Methodist but more tenderly so, with a God of compassion.

Myrtle, much as she appreciated the fellowship of the church and its worship, never became a Methodist. She never joined any church. Like Charles, she was a free and questing soul persuaded that God must surely be a God of love.

Unlike Charles, Myrtle had a sense of parental security. Though the family was by no means wealthy, its church affiliation and the prestige of Marcus Page in the community had societal status. Also, Myrtle excelled as a brilliant student during her school years and showed unusual talent both in writing and elocution. She was given to education, so to say, in a more formal way than Charles' opportunities allowed.

Like Charles, she was an avid reader and seeker in the broad field of religious lore, from spiritualism to the writings of the early church fathers. She absorbed an incredible assortment of books on religion and philosophy, ranging from the writings of early Jewish historian Josephus to biographies of spiritual leaders, such as the Wesleys, Luther, Calvin, and the lives of martyrs and saints.

She was devoted to Shakespeare, Tennyson, and Emerson. It was not only Emerson the essayist who interested her but Emerson the poet. Here was a contemporary of great stature who had written poetically about freedom, faith, reincarnation, and nature's God. The poetic form, the mystical insight of this Unitarian-Transcendentalist intrigued her, for Myrtle was inclined not only toward "poetry that rhymed" but poetic prose as well. The outreach of this innate gift was one day to become part of Unity's treasure of spiritual thought.

Finally, like Charles, she had a fated clinical prognosis engrammed in her mind which was manifested physically. Medical records affirmed that she was consumptive, a disease which, she had been assured, "ran in the family."

Having the Myrtle story in remembrance during my meeting with Charles Fillmore, and knowing how the lines of these two lives were eventually intertwined, I was struck by the utter impossibility of separating the interplay of a divinity that shapes our lives, from chance that dictates conscious choice. If it is true, as I profess to believe, that the point where our talent meets the needs of the world is where God wants us to be, then who or what can move us from that goal?

Consider the story of Myrtle Page during the thirty years before she knew that Charles Fillmore existed. There are times when our life stories seem to write themselves, or when consciousness is the author. We make plans, have secret hopes, project ideas that often fall short of realization. There are fleeting moments of insight when we tell ourselves that even the plans that go astray are necessary for the realization of the larger plan. However it may be, in the case of Myrtle, when her father died in 1865, her assignment was to help assume the responsibilities confronting her mother and family. She was living at home, the love bond between her and Mother Lucy was strong, so her challenge was clear.

Finding employment in Columbus as copy editor and contributing to the "Ohio State Journal," a daily newspaper, she took another forward step in the unfolding story. Two years later came the realization of a seemingly impossible dream: The talented albeit unwell and delicate young woman enrolled in 1867 for literary courses at Oberlin College. This upper Ohio state school was definitely on the religious and social frontiers of the time.

Later in Myrtle's life, her Unity years, she confessed that, "In the field of religious thought, I have always been eclectic!" And that is precisely what Charles Fillmore told me about himself when I talked to him in his Tracy office.

Divine order! There was no accredited college in Myrtle's campus years *more* eclectic than Oberlin. Named in honor of an influential Lutheran philanthropist, Johann Oberlin, who endowed it, it never followed the Lutheran theological line. The college was in essence Presbyterian, but among its founders were Methodists, Congregationalists, Evangelicals, and a former missionary to the Choctaw Indians. Its most famous faculty member, Charles G. Finney, was a "born again" revivalist. The college itself was a way station for fugitive slaves who used the Underground Railroad. It championed the cause of antislavery, in which Myrtle's father had been interested, promoted interracial equality, and pioneered coeducational study at a time when women intellectuals were commonly denounced.

This kind of academic environment left a tremendous impression on a sensitive, cosmopolitan-minded, small-town girl whose talent lay in literary art, whose tastes were esthetic, and whose chosen career was teaching. While she appreciated Methodism and attended Methodist churches, she now found inspiration in the liturgical ritual of the Episcopal faith. The man she was someday to marry was definitely of the same mind. He once said that he was never biased on the God question by an orthodox education!

If divine order was involved in Myrtle Page's registration at Oberlin, it played an equal role during her early years of teaching in a private school in Denison, Texas, an assignment she took because of the climate, which is to say, because of her sickness. The climate in this thriving transportation and cultural center was said to be beneficial for people with constantly threatening "consumptive problems."

So Myrtle went to Denison, and it was here that she was invited one night to a meeting of the local literary club. As the honored guest, she had consented to recite and discuss some of her original poetry. Among those attending this particular colloquium was a young man, a freight office clerk for the Missouri, Kansas, and Texas Railroad. He did not always drop around to these meetings, but on this occasion "by chance" he did. It was an evening in spring during the year of America's first centennial.

This, then, was the way the drama unfolded. For young Charles Fillmore it was a case of love at first sight. In fact, it is reported that Charles, after the meeting, was heard to say, "Someday this woman will be my wife." He supported the prophecy with both letters of affection and date-making in which he revealed his unbounded admiration for the ability and world-wise learning of this captivating, red-haired schoolmistress who seemed to be speaking out of his own heart and mind.

For Myrtle it was the beginning of a romance that evolved ever so slowly and with realistic evaluation of all circumstances, including the health factors of both parties. There was also the age factor, Charles was twenty-two, she was thirty-one, the matter of careers, and many other things. But influencing and recurring in the relationship was an affinity more destined than planned.

There was, for example, Myrtle's involvement in the temperance movement of the time. Her ability to spark the church rallies with her poetry and elocutionary skill got her into the news, into the activism against the "demon rum," and into crusades for getting drunkards, no less than occasional social drinkers, to "sign the pledge and wear the blue ribbon of abstinence" as evidence of a convenant with God.

Charles Fillmore made no bones about the

fact that he occasionally socially imbibed. Nor did he hedge when the bands blared and the ralliers dared converts to the temperance cause to stand up and be counted. He not only stood up, he signed the pledge and soon, with Myrtle at his side, was speaking from the public platform as a dedicated leader in the temperance cause.

The love affair between Charles and Myrtle was a total life adventure. Their courtship covered a period of four years—four fated years, tough years, years of decision, years of economic depression and unforeseen and sudden change. Charles was hindered by his hip condition as the doctors had predicted. Myrtle was still a victim of the "hereditary disease," as medical governance had confidently declared. Each had vocational plans in mind. The letters that passed between them during Charles' various job changes and Myrtle's in-and-out teaching assignments at various posts, were evidence of their love for each other.

In the spring of 1881 they were married in Clinton, Missouri, where Myrtle was teaching. A Methodist minister performed the ceremony in a private home. Their honeymoon was a journey to Gunnison, Colorado, where Charles was involved in a real estate venture, a venture that eventually failed and left him financially strapped, but richer in a profound realization of the indomitable faith, love, and inner power of Myrtle. She became an inseparable adventurer with him in what had become a most difficult and unpredictable period in America's post-reconstruction history. To fortify themselves philosophically against so precarious a world, they turned with fresh inquiry to Emerson and the Transcendentalist teaching that reality is essentially mental and spiritual.

Early in Charles' years of self-appointed studies, an Emersonian concept had been etched in his mind: *There must exist an order of truths which transcends the apparent reach of external cause.* And Charles began thinking more deeply on the availability of that order and those truths for support and help in these times of need.

Caught in the boom and bust lure of real estate, Charles and Myrtle were led to Pueblo, Colorado, for a period of success and failure in the fluctuating land deals rampant in the quixotic and shifting American frontiers. During their three-year stay together in this Centennial State, two children were born: Lowell Page Fillmore in 1882, and Waldo Rickert Fillmore in 1884. The selection of the names is noteworthy. They indicate the trends of thought occupying the minds of the parents at this time. The name "Lowell" was inspired by the contemporary poet James Russell Lowell. "Waldo" was a tribute to the profound influence of Ralph Waldo Emerson on both Charles' and Myrtle's spiritual quests.

The birth of the boys and the maturing of thought were dramatic chapters in the spiraling Fillmore epic. The time would come when it would be hard to imagine the birth of the Unity movement without the birth and influence of Lowell and Rickert. The challenge and speculation about "truth that transcends the reach of external causes," were to represent the cutting edge of the Fillmores' own transcendence. It did not, however, come easily.

A time of major decision lay just ahead when, in the winter of 1884, the family moved to Kansas City, another boom town, another hope and, unforeshadowed, another important upward step in life's spiral climb.

This particular period in the second half of the 19th century was described journalistically as a time when *the Four Horsemen of the Apocalypse are riding roughshod over America.* A case could be made for the metaphor. The horse called *Conquest* was leaving its hoofprints on restless new frontiers. The horseman *Slaughter* graphically typified the final bloody battle between Indians and American troops. The pale horse *Famine* strewed financial panic and depression in its wake. The horse of *Death* ran rampant in the Haymarket riots and bombings in 1886, in the East's worst blizzards in 1888, and in 2,200 victims of the Johnstown flood in 1889.

Within this epochal period the Fillmore family was in dire straits. It is easier to face crises when you are well. Everything appears to be a crisis when you are sick. Charles was not only sick but broke. The Kansas City boom had busted. Myrtle was given little hope for survival because of the advanced stage of her tubercular condition.

A favorite church phrase in vogue during this period of national disaster insisted that "Man's extremity is God's opportunity." The words became an axiom. A cliché. An evangelistic battle cry. It was inevitable that when this saying touched the Fillmore stream of thought it should serve as the consummation for a determined point of resolution.

If God is truly love, does He coerce His children by way of conditions that inflict suffering and death so that they (the children) might be led to His grace and goodness? Was this epigram true? Was this the way in which a benevolent God contrived His "opportunity"? Was the saying logical in the light of reason and truth? Was Myrtle's inherited disease such an extremity, waiting for her to say, "God, this is your opportunity!" Or could it be that *consciousness itself is the ground in which the seed of faith is nourished and broken for one supernal reason:* to learn and to know that God is truly Good, and everything is in divine order?

It was a provocative thought, a thought that would someday be dealt with powerfully in Unity teachings. Everyone talked about God but visualized Him as one who judges and condemns and plagues His children as if chance itself were manipulating the strings of life.

In the stark reality of these years of "God confrontation," Myrtle and Charles supplemented their philosophical convictions with supportive viewpoints from the growing field of New Thought which was going forward under many names: Mental Science, Science of Being, Christian Science, Science and Health, Transcendentalism, and Metaphysics.

Metaphysics was defined as: "Scientific examination of the laws of life, studies of the phenomenon of the human mind, systematic inquiry into the faculties, functions, nature, and attributes of the soul."

Such a coverage was often as complex as the dogmatic assertions and plans of salvation at the orthodox end of the religious spectrum—with one exception: These metaphysical and New Thought approaches were, as a rule, experiential; that is, truths to be tested in experience rather than believed in on ecclesiastical, institutionalized grounds. They represented powers to be used, theories sufficiently open-ended to be explored, leaving room for personal discovery and inner revelations to be tried.

Myrtle and Charles attended meetings whenever possible and read studiously in these fields, and one evening they were guided "as if" by special direction to a person and a place. "As if." In these days there was still an "as if." There was still a resolution to be made about the place of chance and choice in challenges. The birth of Unity at this point was not to come without some special revelation or the expectation of a "miracle."

The place was a meeting hall in Kansas City, the person a certain E. B. Weeks, a teacher at the Illinois Metaphysical College in Chicago, and the year was 1886. Few people knew this speaker, but the college's founder, Emma Curtis Hopkins, was widely recognized as a leader in the New Thought field, a former student and co-worker with Mary Baker Eddy.

At this gathering the speaker included a "healing affirmation" in his lecture and suggested it be used as a working therapy to be taken faithfully, believed in implicitly, and realized fully. The words were: *I am a child of God and therefore I do not inherit sickness.*

For Myrtle it was a moment in which the meeting, the speaker, and the affirmation had irrefutably been established just for her. This was the spiritual prescription for her healing, to be realized through dedication and a technique, faithfully, believingly, and with full realization that *health* was her heritage and not disease.

When I reread the account of how Myrtle's healing eventually took place totally and completely, a healing which was to serve as the power and inspiration for a newborn life in the rise and expansion of a movement called Unity, one truth was clear: The power Myrtle had sought was found within herself. The false and morbid theory that she had been victimized by fate throughout her life, that a disease had been "visited" upon her, was now denied, supplanted by the unshakable knowing that *God is Good,* that God desires good for His children and His world.

Was it actually that simple, that one should merely hear and heed a word, an affirmation, and act upon it after years of struggle, search, medication, and carrying the burden of sickness and the endless hours of despair for so long?

Was it truly that simple, that Myrtle went home from the meeting and said to Charles, "Tonight I have found my answer in Truth. I am a child of God and therefore I do not inherit sickness"?

Was it that simple, that she proceeded daily, often hourly, to manifest the validity of that Truth in her physical body, and that she closed the door and believed that what she sought in secret would be openly revealed, and that she set an empty chair opposite her place of meditation and visualized that Jesus Christ sat across from her and that they communed together in the silence?

Was it honestly that simple, that after several weeks she began to look better and feel better and sense the coming of a new awareness of health and hope in a thrilling expectation of a "miracle"? This was 1889. She did not die but went on to be healed and freed from morbid thoughts about inherited illness and God's wrath and human limitations.

Was it conceivably that simple, that she then became pregnant and gave birth to Royal in 1889—"my royal child," she said— and that he would one day, along with Lowell and Rickert, make a contribution, fill a place in a movement that would encompass the world and that Myrtle herself would live for fifty fruitful years after her healing?

Was it, in fact, that simple?

No. It was that profound. It was so profound that most of us will not believe that mortal mind creates its own false duality with the Mind of God. It is so profound that we refuse to believe in simple terms of love and logic. It is so deeply profound that we are often tricked into insisting that we must not make it simple. Most difficult of all in this profundity is the acceptance of the fact that every moment of life is a convergence point and that we are instruments not only in the growth and healing of *self* but in contributing to the health and development of others.

It was Charles who, seeing the evolving transformation in Myrtle, viewed the "miracle" through his practical mind and took her at her word when she said, "I am healed and you are, too, for we are one!"

That is the way it was.

I saw him at the Unity door on Tracy Avenue. I was with him in his office. I would see him again. As I have said, had you been with me you would not have realized that once he walked with a steel brace, then crutches, then a cane. Now he walked unaided through the rain, alive with life.

He was arranging for me to go to Lee's Summit and see what God was up to at Unity Farm. His son Rick—Waldo Rickert—would show me around the grounds. He was sure I would be interested to see how beautifully things had been timed out there—how the land had waited since the work was halted years before, how the Farm was never really abandoned and the acres were never fallow, though the years were lean; how the seeds of Truth were planted and the fruit was to come forth in its time, as it always does.

I would go tomorrow. Just then I thought of Charles and Myrtle Fillmore when the fullness of time came to them in 1889, the apocalyptic year when they recognized their lives as a manifestation of divine order, and an American faith was born.

Chapter II

The Tower
(Rick)

As I stood in the cupola of Unity tower and looked down at the workmen and machinery moving earth and stone and timber for a village in the making, I was almost hoping that Rick the builder would not come up and join me as he had promised.

He had already taken me over the incredible grounds, the orchards, the lake, the tunnels, and the home called The Arches. Everywhere the scenes were like those of a well-planned country estate. Every person I met seemed to have had a share in this, as if intent on meeting a target date for completion, or, better, a philosophical feeling that there would never be time enough to put together all the creative ideas the master Builder had charted for this kingdom come.

I came to know Rick. I came to understand why his father named him *Waldo* Rickert. Whether he ever used the first name or not is immaterial, it will be said of him as it was of Emerson: *He was ahead of his time. We of the future, rather than those who surrounded him, are his contemporaries. He speaks our language, lives in our scientific age, and addresses himself to the solution of our problems. "Adhere to your own act," he says "and congratulate yourself if you have done something strange and extravagant, and broken the monotony of a conventional age!"*

What Emerson did with words and pen, Rick did with stone and steel and wood and glass. Each in his own way put our relationship to the universe into a new creative perspective.

When I was on these grounds previously in our bogged down car, this tower stood like a lonely sentinel in an unpromised land, despite Papa Charley's hopeful vision of "setting up on earth a bit of the kingdom of heaven."

I was more inclined to believe this prophecy now. Things looked different from the higher altitude than they did from a car, hub-deep in mud and mire. Visions are best known to those who see them from their own perspective and who know the principles needed to project into material reality the blueprints of the mind. One of the principles involved in the building of the tower and the phenomenal construction of what was then called Unity City was the fact that the architect was a son of the founder and that their faith in each other was mutual and sincere.

In my estimation, Rick was the cosmopolite of the Fillmore family. While his father and mother could lay claim to a religious eclecticism, Rick was the eclectic of art and culture. As in their case with spiritual concepts, so Rick in his views of life was not without his own "opinionation." He was an Emersonian man who saw buildings as an expression of worship and who knew that: *There is always some religion, some hope and fear extended from the invisible,—from the blind boding which nails a horseshoe to the mast or the threshold, up to the songs of the Elders in the Apocalypse. But the religion cannot rise above the votary. Heaven always bears some proportion to earth. The god of the cannibals will be a cannibal, of the crusaders a crusader, of the merchants a merchant. In all ages, souls out of time, extraordinary, prophetic, are born, who are rather related to the system of the world, than to their particular age and locality.*

Rick's genius and philosophy, apart from that which was genetic, came from three years of art study abroad, two years at the Art Institute of Chicago, and, by harsh contrast, a year of service in World War I as a corporal in the tank corps. His mind was constantly inventive and full of ideas. Kansas City honored him, and he honored the city by serving as president of the Art Institute, president of the Rotary Club, district governor of Rotary, and host chairman of the Republican Convention held in Kansas City in 1928. But after having spent the morning with him, I had a hunch that those who never saw him on the grounds of Unity, where he crystallized his parents' dream, had never really seen him.

During our exciting tour, whenever we came upon groups of workmen who were turning Rick's ideas into realities, he paused and watched and listened, as if one should never cease learning and never let go of one's own convictions without a challenge. He was at home there. The workers were *his* spiritual family, and that is why I was reluctant to have him come up and take time to stand on the tower with me. He was in charge, always thinking and planning. "I put the men on their own and they get all sorts of wild and wonderful ideas," he told me. "For example, the drought was killing off our walnut trees. They were beauties. Everybody had some opinion about what to do, how to save them, how to deal with the situation. Beautiful trees. But we cut them down and sawed them into boards. Now we have 50,000 feet of black walnut lumber, and it's seasoning wonderfully."

"Speaking of a drought," I answered, "if this is God's work, why a drought?"

"Could be we needed lumber," he mused.

"Seriously, why didn't you dig wells if you needed water?"

"We did dig wells," he admitted blandly, "but we struck oil."

It was true. They struck oil, and natural gas was available for all of the buildings. Unity City was a self-sufficient municipality. It operated its own security force, fire department, and maintenance service. Even the chimes in the tower were built by Unity workers.

I looked out over the terrain and the far country from the open arches of the tower. Somewhere beyond the hazy northwestern miles was Tracy Avenue. Charles Fillmore, I imagined, was busy at his desk or overseeing the printing of some Unity material or sharing his spiritual discoveries with an expectant seeker. In the years ahead he would be coming here with all that constitutes the Unity proliferation, and would consolidate it in this incredible development which now covers more than a thousand acres in the heartland of America. From a rolltop desk to a prophetic bit of heaven on Earth. From a log cabin to a leadership in faith. From "just another man" to a miracle. An American odyssey. An American religion. An American dream.

Below me, approached by winding walks and flowering foliage, was the Silent Unity building. This morning Rick showed me the offices that Charles and Myrtle occupied in the east wing. They used them only for a brief year before that October day in 1929 when money ran out in the America that is always filled with the ebb and flow of material manifestation.

Even after Unity moved back to Tracy and construction in the country was stopped, Myrtle came out a day or two each week to teach, to meditate, and to write. She felt a special nearness to God here, and who wouldn't? The Arches was her "fairyland home," a love gift from Rick as far as the magnificent design and construction were concerned. She chided him and loved him for not putting a kitchen in the many-gabled house with casement windows and an apple orchard setting. But the omission of the kitchen was deliberate. Rick knew she wanted to be free as much as possible and that she felt more called upon to teach and minister than to cook. And, furthermore, Charles' mother—Mother Fillmore, the "grandmother" of early Unity—was the "Martha" who would rather cook than minister. And I asked myself, from my tower point of view, "What is the difference? And who is the more important?" And I got to thinking that Rick had something of both the mother and the grandmother of Unity running through his blood.

And it struck me as interesting that, though I thought of Charles' mother as the "Martha" in the Unity story, her name was actually Mary. Mary Georgiana Fillmore, "Grandma of Unity," who bore Charles in the cabin near St. Cloud before the dawn of the Civil War. And I thought how remarkable it was that she and Myrtle were spoken of by those who knew them as being more like sisters than "in-laws" in their relationship with each other, and how they became one in the spirit of Unity. And how they were both to die in the same year—1931—Mary in March, and Myrtle in October. And how peaceful and natural and quiet were their flights, grandmother of Unity at ninety-seven, and Mother Myrtle of Unity at eighty-six.

From Charles in his study on Tracy to the workers below me in the tracts of this developing city, all seemed part of an inevitable plan which, I told myself with a reached-for conviction, was all in divine order—including me. Which goes to show what magic an observation from an open tower can work in the realm of mind.

An elevator door banged behind me. Rick the architect, the builder, had kept his promise to join me in the tower cupola. Tall, broad-shouldered, genial, a weathered man, in working clothes and a dusty hat, he apologized for being late. His father, he suggested good-humoredly, always made it a point to be punctiliously on time, which was interesting to me, especially in view of the fact that in Unity thinking things are always *in* time anyway, even if you are not *on* time. Rick, I had already realized, was a pragmatist, an inventive genius with a genius' right to his own determined view and eccentricities.

He pointed out various locations of interest with his battered hat, places we visited during our tour: the Silent Unity building, The Arches, the hotel, the footbridge, swimming pool, golf links, tennis courts, the lake, and the orchard.

"Everything here, everything we see, is the

physical counterpart of the spiritual process of the teaching. Father says it is the fulfillment of prophecy."

Filling in certain details, Rick retraced the tour over which he had taken me as if this aerial view imparted a spirit noteworthy on many counts. I shared my enthusiasm by telling him the story I had told Charles Fillmore about my first visit out here and how striking the contrast with the time when the weeds were high and the mud was deep and a propped up sign said, hopefully, UNITY FARM. I said I had felt that at the time the sign needed a question mark.

Rick laughed, then said thoughtfully, "Things developed here the Unity way. That is why some people do not understand."

"Do what you see to do with what you have, and what you need God will supply?" I asked. "Can it be applied to a real estate venture?"

"If it works at all, it works everywhere," Rick declared. "When man works in harmony with God, the right things come at the right time."

Usually when matters having to do with Unity principles came up, as had been true on the morning tour, Rick said, "Talk to brother Lowell about that, or next time you are with

43

Father, ask him. They'll tell you."

Nonetheless, everyone from Charles Fillmore to the workers below us in the busy compound seemed to know about God's law of supply and demand, His system for filling the void and proving one's good. They gave the impression it always worked.

O me of little faith! I thought. Is it possible that the Lord is a spendthrift? Have we in the traditional churches made Him too miserly, too hard to get to for an interview in our needs? Have we fashioned Him too much in our own image and trusted Him, as we often have ourselves, only up to our hip pockets? Or is He actually moving through the Earth seeking those who will exercise an almost arrogant confidence in His generosity?

Swirls of dust rose below us from the torn-up soil in the building area. The whir of machinery increased as Rick explained and pointed out a scene that had all the makings of a movie spectacular. With boyish enthusiasm he described what was going on. I felt the action more clearly than I heard his words. Small crews of men were hoisting massive slabs of concrete out of huge, hulking molds with the aid of ingenious machines. The slabs looked like excavated walls of ancient buildings. They were made to look antique, Rick told me, by a chemical additive in the concrete mixture. One side of the slabs appeared to be pebble-dashed.

Embedded in these huge, rectangular building blocks were steel claws that would be hooked together after the blocks or slabs had been adjusted and set in place. The deft bionic hands of the machines did the adjusting. The slabs were set side by side, horizontally, vertically, or however they were to go. Rick, rarely away from where the action was, seemed to be directing all this mentally for the moment, happy to be there on the tower, yet eager to go down, while workmen in safety helmets climbed alongside the readied walls, lined them up, and locked the steel hooks into place.

Blue flames burst from the blowtorches, welding the retaining claws in the concrete walls. A section of a building sprung up before our eyes. The machines rumbled back, eager to lift another load from the spattered mold. That is how a printing plant was readied, a chapel was constructed, and an administration building took its form.

"Unity City is going up twentieth-century biblical style," Rick told me in a voice that carries its self-fulfilling prophetic note, and he pinned it down with a biblical quote to make it stick, ... *built of stone made ready before it was brought thither...* (I Kings 6:7 A.V.)

I learned later, from a minister in Riverside, California, that Rick realized this prefab-process had the makings of a breakthrough in the building industry. There are those who believe he was the original developer of the prefabrication process in America.

"Why didn't you patent it?" the minister asked Rick. "Why didn't you merchandise it?"

"It was God's idea to begin with," was Rick's reply.

And if I heard correctly, it was Rick's concept of Unity speaking. It was his interpretation, and he had many opinions sociological, ethical, and creative which were *his* views of how Unity principles should be construed. According to Rick, Unity established guidelines and insights to spark creative thought, not to limit it. And Rick knew that his particular "call" was not to philosophize about these "truths" but to express them through his particular talent in architecture and the art of creative building. In this respect, the tower was a symbol.

"Unity," Rick explained, "is like this campanile. Every once in a while some sightseer wants to know what this structure is good for. I make it clear that it is not only a campanile but a water tower. We needed water to run the farm so we made the artificial lake. You saw it this morning. It covers twenty-two acres. When we had the water, we needed elevation and the pressure to distribute it. So we built the necessary tanks and camouflaged them. We are standing on 100,000 gallons of water and six floors of office space."

This was Rick's way of proving the ingenuity of the Unity teachings. As Charles Fillmore had mounted the citadels of American faith and proclaimed: *You cannot use God too often. He loves to be used, and the more you use Him the more easily you use Him and the more pleasant His help becomes,* so Rick, his second son, had enshrined the concept in the tower as a landmark of a new and growing spiritual expression.

Translated into Emersonian language, Rick's approach to architecture could be heard saying, "When a thing has served a useful end to the uttermost, it is wholly new for an ulterior service. In God every end is converted into a new beginning."

I could not help putting myself into a frame of reference at this point. What was actually

47

the real difference between the Unity movement and our traditional Christian denominations? Or, better, what was the underlying power or process that was making it possible for Unity to succeed in its reach for "a bit of heaven on earth" and my unsuccessful one-time try to do something with a church on 36th and Wabash?

Before I got an answer, Rick reminded me that Unity had once had a home on Wabash Avenue, and that his father and mother had lived there in the days when Unity became the name for the work and the movement.

"That," said Rick, "was a long time before the coming of what we are looking at now."

I knew that. I knew about the gabled, two-story house on Wabash and how I had been told that in those early days people used to stop and gawk at the sign that said, "HEALERS AND TEACHERS." It was gossiped about that this was the place where small groups met every evening to sit in silence and "work miracles just by thinking."

That I knew all this was another of the strange coincidences in my relationship with Unity's history. My Wabash church and the Fillmore's Wabash home were part of the paradox no less than the question that stuck in my mind. Why did these newcomers, these

New Thought, mind science, Truth work advocates, generate power and appeal enough to challenge the entrenched religions and then stake out new claims, in this case a Unity City?

I answered part of my question by recognizing that Unity closed a gap between God and the individual—it made God intimate; it met people head-on at the point of human need. I suggested to Rick that perhaps what I and other ministers needed was a Waldo Rickert, a builder, someone who could get dreams onto a drawing board and into reality.

Rick asked simply, "What dream did you have?"

To which I heard myself answer, "I don't know."

"That's the trouble," Rick replied with a shrug and a long, thoughtful look at the scene from the tower.

I should have told him that I did have a sort of dream, my dream, but the timing didn't seem right for the telling, and the plan wasn't clear, and the prompting wasn't there for me to talk about it just then.

I should at least have mentioned in a word that what I had in mind at the Wabash church was something that went back to my own study of Emerson and my fascination with his contention that a reliance on authority marks the decline of religion and the withdrawal of the soul from its highest expression. Emerson contended that numbers do not necessarily count in religion and that God deals with us under no special institutionalized system. I had long had the feeling that what he wrote about and spoke about in his eloquent essay on the *Oversoul* was something that could be extended into an "over-church." What he had foreseen as the free and integrated *person* could be used to create the free and integrated *society* where we would recognize our likenesses and sublimate our differences in the spirit of the quest.

But Rick would probably have said, "That's what Unity is all about, isn't it?"

Perhaps that is why I was held back from bringing up the matter. I was not sure whether that *was* what Unity was actually all about. How would it stand the test of time? Would it turn out to be just another new group, another church, another denomination?

I put the question frankly to Rick. He remained a long time in thought, looking down at the workmen and the buildings. He said what he had said before, "Talk to Lowell about that, or next time you see Father, ask him. They'll tell you."

We stood together in an unforgettable moment and watched the materialization of a structure before our eyes.

"Rick," I said, "that Scripture text, ... *built of stone made ready before it was brought thither...,* where do you find that in the Bible?"

"It's in there somewhere!" he said doggedly.

It was.

I found it in the King James Version, I Kings 6:7 where it is written: *And the house, when it was in building, was built of stone made ready before it was brought thither: so that there was neither hammer nor ax nor any tool of iron heard in the house, while it was in the building.*

Chapter III

The Teachings
(Lowell)

I first met Lowell Fillmore in the early 1940s. His easily accessible office was pointed out to me just off the main lobby in the 917 Tracy building. If the office was easily accessible, so was Lowell. I wondered then and I wonder now whether this genial first son of the founders of Unity had never heard about the image makers' admonition to keep a psychological distance between one's professional self and the public. Isn't it a sign of skill, sinister though it may be, to create the impression you are "hard to get"? Isn't it part of the usual game plan to have a vedette stop you in your tracks with, "Pardon me, sir, do you have an appointment?" Or is it, on the other hand, a touch of greatness to be accessible? Could one of early Unity's secrets of success have been easy accessibility?

In Lowell's case the door was open, he motioned to me to come in, stood up in a gentlemanly gesture, grasped my hand warmly, and invited me to have a chair.

In his early sixties then, handsome, healthy, white-haired, this manager of Unity School of Christianity was an interesting combination of a realistic business executive with the totally unrealistic naiveté of an ancient saint. Though he was in charge of the entire Unity system and its many departments, he seemed to have unlimited time on his hands, as if it were more important that we recognize the feeling of a spiritual unity between us—even if it meant sitting in the silence for a while—than to try to create or force an interrelationship with words alone.

This thought was to remain with me as one of the most significant teachings learned from Lowell as far as human relations were concerned. Let's call it the awareness of a oneness or a unity of spirit. And though I can't for the life of me remember whether the concept was actually spelled out or whether it unfolded gradually in the days ahead, it was, for me, a vital learning, almost something mystical. If there was a mystical ingredient in his father Charles, who had just recently retired from the managerial end of things, Lowell was perpetuating this deeply interpersonal tradition.

The learning was this: You do not try to create a feeling between people; it is self-creative. You do not jockey for positions; the positions are already established. There is always a point of meeting beyond words that takes place naturally by way of an awareness.

It was Lowell who took me in tow and led me deeper into the heart of Unity, whether you wish to interpret Unity as a movement of Spirit or as an American enterprise developing in the matter of the time. Whether I was a researcher or a passerby, a seeker or a cynic, it wouldn't have mattered to Lowell. Unity to him was a mirror in which people saw themselves as they actually were, and in which they recognized what they might conceivably become.

This was my feeling as we started our tour through the Tracy headquarters which in the near future would be replanted to Unity City, later to be called Unity Village.

Lowell, in addition to all I have said of him, was also a bundle of energy. Taking the steps two at a time, he led me up and down through the many Tracy buildings. There was a certain snap and substance about him not usually found in saints, ancient or modern. He wasn't showing off, or was he? No, he was too guileless, too genteel, and too extraordinarily secure. His vitality had something to do with a physical healthfulness as well as a state of mind. Evidently he had some unadulterated secrets to live by. He was a vegetarian. Unlike Rick, who enjoyed a steak and who had a rugged outdoorness about him, Lowell was an indoor type, a quiet nature walk kind of person, quite contented, I learned later, to settle for a vanilla soda, leisurely sipped and thoughtfully enjoyed. Lowell was more in the idiom and discipline of his father who had his mind set on a life span far beyond the statistically established life expectancy. He had the same sense of eternalness stored away in his consciousness as did Papa Charley. Time passes, we stay; or, we stay, time passes. Though everything is in divine order, there are also divine choices.

"Having free will," Lowell insisted, "we can bring our affairs into better order by willingly accepting God's orderly plan."

That was the way Lowell's teaching was focused. And I could not help thinking how thrilling and inescapable the concept of divine order actually is when once you get caught in its implacable net and you begin to feel, as I did when following Lowell, that even two steps at a time may be foreordained, and it is up to your own free will whether you want to interpret the experience as an adventure in exercise or exhaustion!

At any rate, we were now in the printing and publishing department. Here, in the whir of a going concern, the teachings of Unity were being "permanentized." This was big business, bursting the doors and spilling out into the corridors. Outside, the alleys were congested with delivery trucks and mail wagons. I hadn't realized that Unity dominated more than half a block of buildings on Tracy Avenue. Lowell, leading me on, greeting and being greeted by enthusiastic workers, kept saying half to himself, "We've outgrown the place! On to Unity City!"

Wending our way through giant presses, linotypes, and cutting machines staffed by both men and women, we came to a spacious mailing room jam-packed with Unity publications. Here was my first close-up of Unity's bibliography and curriculum. Books! Soft, leather bound books, pocket-sized books, slender books, easy to read, carefully edited books, calling proud attention to titles and authors familiar to an ever-increasing Unity readership that was rapidly becoming international.

"Take your time," Lowell suggested. "Look them over. See how Spirit speaks through the printed word."

The Fillmore name predominated. Just off

the press at the time was Charles Fillmore's *The Twelve Powers of Man.* Also under his authorship, *Talks on Truth, Christian Healing,* and *Prosperity,* and many others. Nearby were a new third edition of *The Healing Letters of Myrtle Fillmore,* and a new edition of *Lessons in Truth* by H. Emilie Cady.

Among the titles I caught a touch of an interesting Unity romance. A book titled *Christ Enthroned in Man* bore the name Cora Fillmore. Nearby was *Teach Us to Pray* by Charles and Cora Fillmore. Cora, who as Cora Dedrick had been Charles' secretary, married Charles Fillmore in 1933, two years after the passing of Myrtle. Charles at the time was seventy-nine; Cora was fifty-seven. They were now, in these 1940s coauthoring books in the field of Unity's teachings.

Thousands of tracts and pamphlets were pigeonholed in long, high shelves. Talk about covering the spectrum of human needs! Had any means of extricating lost humanity from its complexities been overlooked? Not in this labyrinth of leaflets. Even a cursory glance at the titles was convincing: "Demonstrating Prosperity," "Curing the Common Cold Through Forgiveness," "As to Meat Eating," "Casting Out Demons," "Dreams and Their Interpretations," "Health

Through Body Renewal," "Are You Getting All You Want from Life?" "Attaining Immortality," "A Career of Friendliness Is Open to Everyone."

Lowell's name was especially prominent among those timeless tracts. The busiest man on the Unity staff, he was always writing, he told me, because ideas came to him "thick and fast." They expressed themselves in poems and articles that he liked to think were "practical teachings in Truth."

But the richest nuggets from Lowell's mine-of-mind were gathered together under what he called, "Metaphysical Gadgets," affirmations to be empirically proved for their worth in day-by-day situations.

"Try them for yourself," he said, putting the material into my hands. "They can't do you anything but good."

One thing I did find in them, not only at the time but through the years, was that Lowell's "Metaphysical Gadgets" represented Unity's "how-to" programming long before the dawn of America's "how-to" era which was to come some ten years later. Unity was the precursor. Lowell's affirmations had been part and parcel of the Unity lexicon for years, and they were bound to be discovered by the traditional church, as we shall see. His father's writings and his mother's publications were seedlings for the eventual "how-to" harvest yet to come.

"Metaphysical Gadgets" suggested: When you have mislaid something and feel yourself distraught, affirm: *There is nothing lost in Spirit.* In winning friends, hold to the thought: *I am a radiating center of divine love.* Should a gossip or a bore mooch on your time, assure yourself that: *No one cometh unto me save the Father has sent him.* When answering the doorbell and you are in a dash, or when you see someone coming at you through the crowd and you are in a hurry, repeat silently: *I go to meet my good.* Confront that gloom-and-doomer who enjoys telling you that you are not looking up to par with the positive conviction: *I am Spirit and Spirit cannot be sick.* If you are caught in a storm or distressed by noise, affirm: *Peace, be still.* For heart flare-ups repeat believingly: *My heart is right with God.*

After reading some of these I said to Lowell, "Is it correct to say that Unity aims at a personalization of religious truths and at a popularization of religious mysticism?"

His answer was instantaneous, "Unity aims at a constant realization of the Christ within."

That was what I had been hearing ever since my meeting with Charles Fillmore—even before that—ever since my reading of Myrtle Fillmore's dramatic healing. What is the Christ within but the discovery and conviction that *I am a child of God?* I had heard it as a cardinal Unity precept ever since I met Rick, who, as far as I was concerned, manifested the truth of the indwelling Christ by transmuting creative thought into structured things. I had heard about this manifesting of the divine nature, the Christ-in-you belief in Unity centers everywhere. Everywhere, the lessons were built around the Christ consciousness. It was the key designed to open new doors of understanding to the true nature of Self. Unity was pointing out that this key is found not only by way of affirmation, but in meditation, prayer, inner quiet in silent unity with God.

Just now, however, the metallic whir of the restless presses told me a different story. They were raising noisy argument over the contention that the most powerful teachings of Unity are generated in inner stillness. It was as if the printery was saying, "Here is where the power and growth of Unity are found! Through us a million monthly readers are learning about the everyday use of the

Christ principle!"

Where are these readers, the Unity followers? I learned from Lowell that most of them were not even Unity members. How many Unity centers are there? At that time, in the mid 1940s, there were 110 Centers with an estimated membership of some 10,000. And how many subscribers to Unity publications? More than 400,000. That was the picture of Unity coming through to me. It was a movement making its way into the hearts and homes of churched and unchurched people of all denominations. Unity was ministering to both a visible and an invisible congregation.

Foremost among the publications was DAILY WORD, the famous "word for today" devotional reading. Here was UNITY, a magazine of Christian metaphysics for whoever was interested in the subject; *Weekly Unity,* designed for sincere Truth seekers everywhere; *WEE WISDOM,* a magazine for children under the age of thirteen no matter what church or what culture they belonged to; *Good Business,* success stories attesting to the effectiveness of Unity's teachings in the business world; *Progress,* positive-thinking stories for young people in any walk of life.

The incessant drone of the printing establishment had a right to say, "The printed word is the secret behind Unity's success!" Understandably, machines and those who operated them, laying page on page, folding, cutting, binding, shipping, would be justified in claiming: "*We* are the endless voice of Truth!"

But then, suddenly, a gong sounded above the clattering presses. A workman pulled a switch. The presses stopped. Busy human hands paused instantly in their work. The huge room quieted. Throughout the working area, silence. Throughout the building, silence. Men and women everywhere within the sound of the gong halted in their tracks and were silent. Lowell stood, eyes closed, hands folded as if in prayer. I was inspired to do likewise. The silence, deep and sincere, that hung over us was now quietly broken by a voice transmitted over a loudspeaker, Charles Fillmore's voice, consecrating and blessing the work of Unity. This was followed by a dramatic pause, and then the prayer: *Our Father who art in heaven, hallowed be thy name. Thy kingdom come, Thy will be done....* " (Matt. 6:9)

Perhaps I was wrong. Perhaps an inner silence is the voice of Unity—not books, not tracts, not periodicals—silence. A flow of thought. An awareness. A state of consciousness. The Christ within.

We walked for quite a while in silence after that, thinking our own thoughts. Lowell informed me that this "prayer-break" was a daily inclusion in the work at headquarters. It was his father's idea. It had already become a tradition.

We went into an office devoted to a work called Silent-70, a department responsible for the distribution of free Unity literature to military bases, hospitals, prisons, orphanages, libraries, institutions for the blind, and other humanitarian social centers. Begun in 1910, it was built on the inspiration of Luke 10:1: ... *the Lord appointed seventy others and sent them ... into every town and place* ... Now, some thirty years later, it had not seventy but more than 7,000 volunteers who took care of this literature distribution, 500,000 pieces per year, all supported by freewill contributions.

Commenting on my impression that Unity was a highly commercial enterprise, Lowell made it clear that from the inception of Unity in 1889 it was a Fillmore policy not to charge for spiritual services. From the very time of their healings, Charles and Myrtle affirmed and put into practice the determination that,

"The work is the Lord's and He will provide the means for its propagation."

I was to pursue this more because of persistent claims by outsiders and traditional church leaders that the Fillmores were supplementing the working of divine principles with promotional ingenuity typically Americanesque. Of course, traditional churches were doing this, too, and may therefore have been more sensitive—and hopeful—that the newcomers were bathing in the same stream, so to say.

There was, however, an unusual phenomenon in the Fillmore enterprising. I refer to a certain "Dedication and Covenant." Whether Lowell knew about it at the time of our meeting, I do not know. I did not ask him, because I knew nothing about it. It is said that no one knew anything about it until 1942. But the document bears strongly upon the basic thrust of Unity's founders and their ideological approach to partnership with God in Unity's work on planet Earth.

The "Dedication and Covenant," found among the Fillmore writings and effects, is not only important in the history of Unity, it presents food for thought to spiritual leaders and religious movements everywhere. It cuts through the profit motive with the razor's edge of Truth that God does indeed respond as a law of cause and effect and with an element of love to those who take Him at His word.

Written in 1892, in circumstances we can only imagine but in a spirit undeniably sincere, Charles and Myrtle composed and signed a pact which said:

"*We, Charles Fillmore and Myrtle Fillmore, husband and wife, hereby declare ourselves, our time, our money, all we have and all we expect to have, to the Spirit of Truth, and through it, to the Society of Silent Unity.*

"*It being understood and agreed that the said Spirit of Truth shall render unto us an equivalent for this dedication, in peace of mind, health of body, wisdom, understanding, love, life and an abundant supply of all things necessary to meet every want without our making any of these things the object of our existence.*

"*In the presence of the Conscious Mind of Christ Jesus, this 7th day of December, A.D. 1892.*"

As has been said, the unearthing of this

"Dedication and Covenant"—now displayed in many Unity centers and ministers' studies—was unknown at the time of my meeting with Lowell. However, this makes doubly significant the nearness of Lowell's thought and teaching in regard to prosperity and God's munificence.

He left no doubt in my mind that God is a most generous dispenser of inexhaustible good, and that He is a Partner to be contracted with or at least one who is open to covenanting. This means that not only the virtues expressed in the "Dedication and Covenant"—peace of mind, health of body, wisdom, and the like—but also material substance that pays the rent and buys the land and keeps the presses rolling are involved in a divine partnership. God the Partner is no miserly Giver, and His children, according to Lowell and Unity teaching, should be no small requesters. And above all, they should be willing to accept their good!

"If you are hungry," says Lowell, "you can just as well ask for a square meal as for a crust of bread. The divine invitation is, '*Ask, and you shall receive.*' Jesus Christ said, 'Whatsoever you shall ask in my name, that will I do, that the Father may be glorified in the Son. If you ask anything in my name, that will I do.' When we ask for a pittance we usually do so because we feel that there is not enough for all. This feeling shows that our faith in God's inexhaustible abundance is weak. All things in nature have been provided lavishly. More seed is produced by plants than the soil can accommodate. Compared with the universe of stars and space, our Earth is as small as a speck of dust, and compared with the size of the Earth, our personal needs are infinitesimally small. Limitation is in our own capacity to receive. The very fact that we cannot ask largely proves that our capacity is limited."

Hearing Lowell speak along these lines and reading the written words in his teachings, I looked at him again. Feeling the humble greatness of his presence, I was tempted to say, "Who and what is the real Lowell Fillmore?"

Is he a guileless child of his covenanting father and mother, or one who rationalizes riches as the greatest gift of the Christ within? Where does the real Lowell stand in the bewildering equation of the selfless Galilean who now suddenly wants His followers to be rich in the coin of the realm? It was a question conjured up by my years of orthodoxy. It was a question for which an answer would be forthcoming. But just now it was profoundly important in my work and research. The longer I was with Lowell, the oftener I met him, the more his Unity keys fit into many of my traditional dilemmas. Lowell was largely responsible for wisely approaching me on the basis of interest in paradoxical reasoning.

Not everyone would agree or needed to agree, but the paradox was this: The more Lowell visualized his good, the more he realized it in consciousness, if not in actuality. Consciousness, however, became, for him, actuality itself as far as his life and thought were concerned.

He had what he felt he had, and having it in the essence of feeling he did not crave it in materiality. It was a mystical approach, a possession in Spirit, truly his, and to those who understood the paradox, Lowell's teaching was understandable. Somewhere in this, as far as I was concerned, was a verification of the promise that to those who have, more shall be added.

Lowell put it this way, "If you were to pray, 'God give me a million dollars,' you probably would not get it because you would not have faith that you would get it, and you would not have the ability to use it wisely. It would be much wiser to pray for wisdom, love, and understanding enough to be able to appreciate a million dollars. We need to pray for a greater capacity to live and understand life. God has already given us more than we are using. We must first learn to use what we already have."

Here, then, was the imperceptible line between the value of money and the love of it, a teaching not easy, not always clear. It is understood best by way of stewardship and a sense of values as over against dominance and a sense of possession. It is seen most clearly in the person involved, as I was seeing it in Lowell. He was a rich man, but not in material riches. He was one of God's spiritual millionaires.

I was to meet him many times in the years ahead and think of him often. In fact, I thought of him in Japan when, among the Buddhist devotees of Sojiji temple, I asked one of the chief disciples how he maintained his peace and poise in the midst of the rush and turmoil of life to which he was continually subjected during his days in the workaday world. He said to me that if there was any secret it was merely that he never left his *place of meditation*. He meant that, although he was physically occupied elsewhere, his mind and consciousness were always in his center of spiritual orientation. He never left it, and it never left him.

There was something of this process of bilocation in Lowell. Wherever he was, he was never far from his place of oneness with God. God did not create a psychological distance between Himself and His children. God was easily accessible, open and free. This impressed itself upon me so much in my meeting with Lowell that I construed it as a quality inherent in the entire Unity community.

And about this I was to learn more, as we all do, by divine order, in the days ahead.

Chapter IV

The Window

The coming of light, whether in the sense of the solar system that lights the world or in terms of a spiritual light that illumines the mind, is symbolized in Unity by a lighted window.

Unity did not set out to create this imagery, for Unity is not particularly interested in the use of signs or symbols. The popularity of the window was self-developing. It simply grew, and through the years became recognized as representing the epicenter of the Unity way of life.

But at this point, it is difficult for me not to mention a grand analogy, a symbolism, if you will, quite irresistible. Consider how many candles were lighted, how much oil was burned, how many wicks were trimmed in lamps since prehistoric times, how many lamplighters carried torches to light the lights in streets and market places and cathedrals. Think of how much research was done and how many dreams were dreamed before a little man in Menlo Park, New Jersey tied

73

some silken strands inside a fragile tube and said, "Let's have more light!"

That was in 1882. The man was Thomas A. Edison. The place where the miracle was demonstrated to the world was New York City, on Pearl Street, to be exact. The new light was the incandescent bulb.

Now, consider how many religions came to America, how many sermons were preached, how many utopian experiments were tried, how many prophecies foretold, how many attempts were made to convert the "heathen," and how many rituals and revivals were designed to "save the sinners" before a husband and wife founded a new spiritual work and said, "Let's have more light on the limitless power of God!"

The place was Kansas City. The location, an upper room in the Fillmore home at 641 Wabash. The new spiritual light was the Society of Silent Help, started in 1890 (now Silent Unity).

Incidentally, the first incandescent bulb was brought into Kansas City in 1886 by humanitarian Edwin B. Weeks. (The same year E. B. Weeks brought the "light" of the healing message to Myrtle Fillmore.) The bulb was a great attraction in his private office, greater by far than the gaslight which

74

burned in the upper room of the Wabash home. Early in the 1890s incandescent bulbs made their debut in most Kansas City homes, and one burned each night in the upper room on Wabash where prayers were said and the presence of God was made real. Kansas City was one day to be recognized as "the first American city to have gone totally electric." That is a fact little known even today. The fact of the lighted window is now known universally.

I wrote about Unity and its window in several church publications in the 1940s, "Christian Century," "The Expositor," and others, suggesting how far the penetrating rays of the Unity light were beginning to extend. The articles got something off my chest: the intransigence of churches like my early church on Wabash refusing to investigate or recognize what had happened in a house on the same street in the late 1880s, and what its implications were to be for the religion of our time.

What *was* happening in that maverick movement referred to as "Fillmoreism" way back when?

Well, for one thing, there was this small, solid group of seekers, New Thought and Divine Science people, friends of the Fillmores for the most part, who met with Charles and Myrtle nightly to channel the healing power of faith and prayer to whomever or wherever they fixed their minds.

The Fillmores had personal proof that the power existed, that it was public domain, and that it worked: Myrtle had been healed. Her healing inspired Charles to utilize the same spiritual therapy for his withered leg and his afflicted hip. Charles was of the opinion that the principles would have to prove their worth for him or they were fraudulent.

He began his treatments with a technique largely his own, but patterned on Myrtle's approach and conviction: *Disease has no place in life as a permanent reality, perfect health is inherent in Divine Mind, the Christ in you is the hope of healing.*

Charles sought a quiet place where he could enter into the silence. Waiting upon God, he discovered he could send spiritual impulses to any part of his body. He once described these sensations to me as "crawly feelings." Each day he applied the impulses to his afflictions, affirming health, thinking health, drawing upon the promises of Jesus Christ to "ask and receive," recognizing his own perfection as a "child of God," and seeking to develop the faith that would "work the healing."

The silence became his covenant with universal Mind. He began getting messages. Open to vibrations and new states of consciousness, he insisted he was "growing new tissue." His leg was lengthening. He no longer used the steel brace he had worn since boyhood. He discarded his cane. He was beginning to demonstrate a complete "body regeneration," and Scripture supported him with a promise: *... be transformed by the renewal of your mind...* (Rom. 12:2) In Fillmore's reasoning the process was *the release through direct affirmations of electronic forces sealed up in the nerves.*

He felt he was at the heart of a gigantic discovery. Ideas grew wild and fast in his active mind. Throughout his life, he decided, he had been battling windmills of fate when all he needed was to enter the mystical calm of his own soul. God worked from the inside out. Life suddenly became adventurous. The awareness of the Christ presence was becoming real. With Myrtle at his side, he believed they had captured a force that could beat back and conquer whatever doubt or prejudice might stand in their way. An unshakable belief developed that they were being led into a full and complete realization of the kingdom of God. Charles referred to this conviction as the "Christ-Power," and upon this fundamental belief the Society of Silent Help was built.

So they invited people to come and sit with them in prayer during these night sessions so that they, too, could become channels of healing, messengers of light. Their monthly magazine, *Modern Thought,* started in 1889, invited seekers to join in this grand adventure. The magazine suggested affirmations—virtue words, words of power upon which to meditate, thoughts to polarize one's faith.

To many in those days who saw the lighted window from the outside, the concept was all too simple. It was not only too simple, it was heretical. But it wasn't enough of an issue to cause concern among leaders or people of the church-at-large. After all, here were a few dozen odd-minded people meeting in a home, sitting in the quiet, singing a song or two, cozying up to God. This was not a church, and how can you have a true religion without one? There were no ordained minister, no ritual, no tradition, no sacrament. They didn't even take up an offering. They didn't even have a name.

Nor was there any particular public attention paid to the fact that with reports of healings and a sense of dedication, the Society of Silent Help was now securing a hall for its meetings. The hall could accommodate some 200 people who, regardless of sect or creed, were invited to join in the search and discovery of "Truth." The attendance grew. Myrtle and Charles were looked upon as healers and teachers. The silence at the evening sessions was as fervent as that of early Christian Pietists, the testimonies as emphatic as those of early Methodism, the terminology smacked of Christian Science, and hints of the supernormal were in the line of Christian mysticism.

It came more as a source of wonder than surprise when at one of the meetings Charles Fillmore broke the silence with an excited exclamation, "Unity!" And as the members of the group opened their eyes questioningly, he repeated the word, *Unity! That's the name for our work, the name I've been waiting for!*

Unity, he elaborated, *embodies the central principle of everything we believe. Unity of the soul with God, unity of all life, unity of religions, unity of body and mind, unity of all people in the search for Truth.*

To those who later accused Fillmore of having "thought up" a good name, he parried by saying the word came to him: "... *as clear . . . as though somebody had spoken to me.*"

The name *Unity*—ahead of its time as we view it from our modern perspective—almost instantly metamorphised The Society of Silent Help into Silent Unity. *Modern Thought* magazine became UNITY Magazine. A Unity Book Company was established. In 1903 the word *Unity* was legally incorporated and chartered for the purpose of demonstrating "Universal Law."

No modern religion had a more laborious beginning. Every step of the way had been built on faith in a miracle, or belief in revelation, or a demonstration of both. Every early devotee seemed to demand a special proof of God's presence, a victory over a problem, a believable answer to prayer, a healing of some physical need. Every publication of the magazine was a venture into the confused and obdurate stream of prejudice from those who prejudged "Fillmoreism" in the light of Christian orthodoxy. Nor did it help to bridge the prejudicial gap when Fillmore was heard to say, "He who writes a creed or puts a limit to revelation is the enemy of humanity. Creeds have ever been the vampires that sucked the blood of spiritual progress in the past, and life can only be kept in the present moment by latitude of thought tempered always by the power that moves the world, namely Love!"

The centripetal force of the electrifying word *unity* began putting it all together. *Silent Unity* was far more descriptive than *Silent Help*. It suggested a unification with traditional Christianity as the life of Jesus had demonstrated it and as the Christ had proved it. The new name, Unity School of Practical Christianity, put the organizational plan squarely on the line. Unity was the goal as well as the path to the goal. The designation *School* made it clear that the program was geared to teaching and living the Word rather than preaching and professing the Word. The key phrase, "Practical Christianity," reiterated the belief that the Jesus Christ way is timeless, that religion has a living function, and that faith and prayer operate in accordance with the believer's will to believe. "Truth principles," as Fillmore had said before his healing, "must prove their worth or they are fraudulent."

Though the Fillmores had shied away from creeds, believing with Emerson that they *check, crib and confine the thoughtful mind,* they were accused of becoming doctrinaire at this point in Unity's history when they pro-

81

claimed: "Whatever man wants he can have by voicing his desire in the right way into universal Mind." It was a thought that could easily be interpreted as being beyond pure Emersonian thinking. If the words did not constitute a creed, they certainly suggested a most grandiloquent promise.

And Unity was to have a universal symbol whether it wanted it or not: a lighted window which, as we shall see, was to find its permanent home wherever Unity's headquarters were destined to be.

Making it clear that they had no quarrel with the "mental cure" groups, or with what they had learned from Christian Science, New Thought, and all the rest, the Fillmores insisted that Unity was premised on a power higher than the intellect. This power demanded freedom, freedom of thought, openness to new revelations, and the right, as Myrtle emphasized, to new perspectives of thought as religious truths matured. Or, as Charles Fillmore once told his students, "I reserve the right to change my mind!"

Institutionalized Christendom could, obviously, never allow sufficient latitude for such open-ended thinking. "That kind of wine," a preacher friend of mine told me, "was much too new for our old bottles." And

Fillmore said, "The churches talk a great deal about God and about the *past* experiences of the prophets and saints, but the present power of God has seemed to have disappeared from their midst. We feel that we are to bring in a new dispensation with the Power of Spirit." It was a daring challenge in those days because it was bringing a religious ethic ever closer to the maelstrom of the "life of the world." It is still a daring challenge. It always will be. Can a new dispensation persuade a secular society to conform to spiritual truths without distilling truth to a point of convenient societal acceptance? It was and continues to be a most intriguing question.

But one thing was certain. The Unity light was there, the lighted window was for real, and the secret of sending spiritual power into the secular world on the wings of Silent Unity was impressive. The technique employed by Silent Unity was by no means new. It had been used by the earliest Christians when they met in their "upper rooms." It had been employed by every group of devotees who sincerely believed and practiced the basic text, "... *where two or three are gathered in my name, there am I in the midst of them.*" (Matt. 18:20)

Silent Unity's enactment of this promise

was to prove beyond the shadow of a doubt the metaphysical principle that: *Dedicated service working in harmony with universal Spirit leads inevitably to consecrated goals.*

The continuity of Unity as a new spiritual science movement was now clear. The Silent Unity sessions in the Fillmore home generated their own consciousness. Spectacular reports began circulating: A laundress was cured of asthma; a cripple on crutches was healed; a boy threatened with blindness received his sight.

Testimonies spread. Doubters came to sit in the prayer circle. Skeptics fanned the publicity with accusations of superstition, magic, animal magnetism, and downright fraud. The evening meetings moved to a larger public hall. The popularity of Silent Unity spread by word of mouth, by means of the printed word, and by the pulling power of faith and prayer.

Letters were soon coming in from people unable to attend the meetings, all sorts of people who had been alerted by some sort of mental messengering or the subtle nudging of Spirit. Silent Unity workers began blessing the letters and letting the writers know they, too, were being blessed.

Myrtle Fillmore, mystically minded,

motherly at heart, sincerely dedicated, held the letters prayerfully between her hands, visualizing the writers and surrounding them with love and light. The workers made the practice part of their program. Charles agreed. At the start, when letters were relatively few, they were passed among the circle of workers who affirmed God's presence with the sender. When correspondence reached flood stage, the letters were blessed en masse—in the mail bags. So were the answers, answers carefully prepared, suggesting usable affirmations, constructive advice, and assurances of love.

Telephone calls kept pace with the rising tide of mail. Whenever possible, Charles and Myrtle personally answered the calls. Originally they had a night line, so to say, close to their sleeping quarters. This was the forerunner of the round-the-clock Silent Unity telephone service, first in the Fillmore home, then in a room on the top floor of the building on Tracy where, in a previously unused office, God's answering service was staffed by Silent Unity workers. Interestingly, dramatically, the light in this upper room was to become a conversation piece. People began talking about the lighted window. You had to look up to see it. It reflected its light through a small, ordinary window, but it had the appearance of great antiquity. It was always there. The constancy of its light and the references to miracles caught people's imagination.

The lighted window was still there during my visit in the 1940s when Silent Unity was also preparing to move back to Unity Farm—Unity Farm, Unity City, Unity Village or Unity Headquarters, the names were interchangeable. An average of 1,000 letters a day were pouring into the spiritual nerve center in the Tracy building. Telephone calls, letters, telegrams, and occasional raps at the door were evidence of the drawing power of the abiding insistence in American life that there is always someone at this spiritual port qualified to give help at a time when help is needed.

God knows that help was needed in the decade of the 1940s. These were the years introduced with the proclamation of the Four Freedoms, and they were to go down in history as years of testing as to freedom's durability on any score. These were the years of World War II, Pearl Harbor, Midway, the atom bomb, Hiroshima, and Nagasaki.

The Silent Unity telephone number in those days was Victor 8720. I can attest that during my Unity stay the nature of the prayer requests was quite apart from the maelstrom of war, politics, and atomic devastation. Evidently there was a feeling in American society, as there was in my heart and mind, that global situations can become so colossal, so beyond the reach of reason, that they seem beyond the reach of prayer; as if it might be an affront to God to draw His attention to man's repeated cry of "peace through bloodshed," or what Emerson once described as, *the epidemic insanity of war.* The calls coming in to Silent Unity were deeply personal, as they have continued to be. They dealt, not with the issues that form the flow of recorded history, but with the individual's relationship with the Great Unknown. Sometimes tragic, sometimes frivolous, the pleas were always human, in the eternally searching perspective of God-and-me.

Victor 8720! A midnight plea from a dormitory in a state university: "I need help. I am going blind. The doctors say they can do nothing. Can you help me?"

Victor 8720! A young wife explains that her husband is an airline pilot. "He is overdue at the airport. He is flying in bad weather. He needs your guidance."

Victor 8720! A businessman is negotiating

an important transaction: "I must have prosperity thoughts. Please send them through at two o'clock eastern standard time!"

Day and night it went on. Around the clock there was always someone on duty in the lighted room to answer, "Silent Unity. What can we do for you?"

Affirmations and spiritual advice appropriate to the needs of those who called were transmitted over the telephone and by letter. Equally important was the fact that within the gathering of Silent Unity workers themselves prayers were spoken and a spirit of positive solution for problems was evident in their work.

In the 1940s, 120 men and women were involved with the Silent Unity service. Their influence was reaching across the spiritual horizons of America. The number of workers was multiplied many times by others in the Unity ministry and throughout the Unity movement who were affirming health, prosperity, spiritual illumination, and social adjustment. The thousands of letters being answered covered every conceivable subject that plagues or prospers humankind.

I well remember the morning I stopped in at the third floor chapel at 917 Tracy, a place fittingly dedicated to this Silent Unity ministry. In a nearby office an elderly gentleman sat at a telephone. In adjoining rooms Silent Unity workers were stuffing envelopes with pamphlets and mimeographed form letters done in purple ink. A woman worker told me that purple was a symbol of spiritual power.

I asked for and was given one of the letters. Directed to people who had made requests for physical healing, it read:

Dear Friend,

You cannot know with what faith and love and joy we send this assurance, 'You are not alone. God is with you.' This is true. There is no aloneness—God is all. Use the enclosed words of prayer: "THE HEALING POWER OF GOD THROUGH CHRIST IS NOW DOING ITS PERFECT WORK IN ME, AND I AM MADE WHOLE." For God's healing power is at work. See His perfection made manifest in mind and body.

In healing faith,
Silent Unity

Silent Unity, motivated by a desire to help people in an invisible fellowship of faith, was working so successfully that I wondered why every minister, whatever his or her church, did not install a "lighted window." Was there actually this much power in the Word, even in a semi-personalized set of words? Was it as simple as this?

It wasn't. Looking at Unity we had the mistaken idea that the entire structure of the movement was simply another American success story. The catch was that we of the traditional church did not realize that *this new thought religion differed from the old time religion in its emphasis on the creative power of Mind.* And our age was moving into an intensive era of new thinking on the basic dogmatic assertions about God, Christ, salvation, sin, suffering, heaven and hell, good and evil, health and sickness, prosperity and poverty, Christians and non-Christians, inner light and outer reality, and the tantalizing touch of miracles.

People were calling Silent Unity as if they had gotten hold of God's unlisted telephone number. At last they had an open line. When they mailed in their prayer requests they were meeting faith halfway, and it often seemed as though God's good angels were already reading their thoughts. In fact, a physician said to me, "If people had the faith in me that they have in Silent Unity, their healing would be considerably easier and surer."

But there was one thing more about the Silent Unity mystique overlooked by the church-at-large, by the medical profession-at-large, and by society-at-large. It came in the form of a pocket-sized booklet plainly and simply titled DAILY WORD.

Born in 1924 as the brain child of Frank B. Whitney, its first editor, DAILY WORD bore the spirit or the incarnation, if you will, of thoughts and affirmations utilized years earlier in the development of Unity. At that time, *Modern Thought* magazine suggested words to live by and positive statements to be used at the meetings of the Society. This was an approach now brought into full flower in DAILY WORD, and the publication was to become the most influential child of Silent Unity and the entire Unity movement.

Innovative and inspiring, DAILY WORD expressed in modern form an idea which had been used in religious lore ever since medieval times when the early church fathers found spiritual guidance in what they called "the Offices" or "The Litany of the Hours." These were prescribed readings for deepening spiritual consciousness, and an indispensable part of the traditional training of candidates for Holy Orders and the Christian vocation.

There has always been an inner need in the

human life for guidelines to be followed *daily* in the way of religious discipline. Human nature being what it is, both human and divine, desperately needs some special daily nourishment besides food and drink—a spiritual supplement. Unity, with characteristic practicality, approached the need from its customary premise that by affirming spiritual reality, human unrealities find their proper sublimation, and life is put in balance and in tune.

So here was DAILY WORD, prepared to perform precisely what it professed, a prestigious daily affirmation, insightfully interpreted and supported by a relevant biblical text. The impact was instantaneous. Making its debut in the affluent mid-1920s, DAILY WORD grew and prospered through the years of the Depression, the Depression's aftermath, and now, in the 1940s, its circulation was nearing 300,000.

Its readership could be estimated at double or triple that number because it was already becoming a family devotional reading as well as the bearer of a personalized message. Executives had it on their desks, subscribers represented all walks of life, and people who requested copies and could not afford the one dollar a year subscription received DAILY

WORD without cost. So did hospital patients, elderly citizens, and prison inmates.

The editor of DAILY WORD in the mid-1940s was Martha Smock. I was to meet Martha later in her remarkable career.

In this period of Unity's move back to the Farm I had my first of many visits with Silent Unity's legendary May Rowland. Our paths were to cross through the years, at Unity headquarters, in her home on Unity Ridge, and one special morning when she asked me to speak to her group of workers in the prayer ministry of Silent Unity. It was a peak experience, as it must be for anyone who catches the consciousness of those who channel the prayer power literally throughout the world.

I recall particularly a visit with May in the consultation room following that meeting. The room had been built originally for Charles Fillmore. Its tranquillity left no doubt in my mind that God dwells most vividly in the calm. The quiet surroundings, the simple, stately chairs, table, and hearth were just right for the setting, and May Rowland was just right for the Unity program. Through more than half a century of service, she was to be a symbol of Silent Unity's inner calm, an example of those who have learned to still certain senses, to hush certain impulses, to maintain a sensitive sense of humor, to enfold in a mystic kind of serenity the circumstances which so easily toss most of us about.

Of course, what May might or might not have known is that she herself, human, vibrant, mortal, as we all are, was a charismatic bearer of the infectious light of Truth. In the serious business of life, and in dealing with those who walked the edge of need and often tragedy, May never lost either her impenetrable reach of understanding or her remarkable poise. But, then, that is what Silent Unity and the lighted window are all about.

Fittingly and beautifully, after May's departure into the greater Light in early April 1977, it was decided by Unity officials that there should henceforth be a special DAILY WORD edition in memory of May and her loyal dedicated service. This edition is now in a large print, easy to read publication for those who need it and want it.

One day I read through the very first copy of DAILY WORD in the Heritage Room in the ever-expanding Unity School library. The copy, dated July 1924, was in every way the harbinger of things to come. The dedication was: *To the daily practice of Christian Truth.*

One cannot read this first edition without sensing the dynamism in which Spirit moves between the reader and Silent Unity. It is here we realize that the *people* and the Unity program are inseparable and that DAILY WORD is the extended light of the lighted window. In its very first "Word for Today" this introductory copy said:

God in me is my light and my understanding.

The truth that God is the Father of man does away with the oft-proclaimed presumption that it is impossible for the finite to understand the Infinite.

The lesson topic in this first edition was titled "Christian Healing," and it said:

In order to have spiritual understanding, man must first realize that he has capacity for it. When one acknowledges that it is natural and right for man to have full knowledge of the Infinite, he is but confirming his own ability to enjoy infinite understanding. Man is the manifestation of God within, and, in His likeness, is all-wise and all-knowing.

To believe in the real presence of God as Divine Mind in you is to identify yourself with all light and knowledge. Man is primari-

ly mind and is necessarily unlimited mentality. He takes his God-given dominion and power first through consciousness, and, consequently, must have full possession of all truth.

Begin today to rise out of the belief that by nature you are limited in understanding. Never think or say that anything is too difficult for you to comprehend. Think at all times of man as capable of knowing all truth. Learn to rely upon the light of God within to make clear whatever you wish to know.

"God, who commanded the light to shine out of darkness, hath shined in our hearts, to give forth the light of the knowledge." (A.V.)

"The earth shall be full of the knowledge of Jehovah."

So ended the reading. But, for the movement called Unity, it was only the beginning.

Chapter V

The Ministry

Sow a new seed of faith in the public mind and you reap a church.

This anonymous axiom cannot be pinned on Emerson, as some would wish. He would likely have prefaced it with *Beware!* as he did in his famous saying: *Beware when the great God lets loose a thinker on this planet. Then all things are at risk!*

By reason of many similarities no less than differences, Ralph Waldo Emerson and Charles Fillmore occupied a certain togetherness in my mind during the 1940-1960 period when the metaphysical movement was rapidly expanding across America. Truth students were referring to Emerson as the father of New Thought and to Fillmore as the father of Unity.

Emerson, a Harvard graduate, had been ordained in his day by the Unitarians, served a New England Unitarian Church for three short years, and astounded his parishioners by resigning on grounds of intellectual and spiritual conflicts. He felt he needed freedom in both fields, spiritual and intellectual, in order to reconcile idealism and materialism as being complementary and not competitive.

Fillmore, self-educated for the most part, unordained by traditional standards, championed freedom of thought, left it open-ended, and lifted idealism to such a height that it carried materialism along with it until it too became spiritualized.

Emerson, though he might not have admitted it, was one of the thinkers let loose by God, and he was to have a following whether he liked it or not. Fillmore sowed a new seed of faith in the public mind, and he was now destined to reap a church whether he wanted it or not.

Both men were highly eclectic, open to constructive thought whether it came out of scriptures or societies, old or new. Both bet their lives on the immutability of moral and spiritual law. Both felt the need for nearness to nature in the spiritual quest, whether, as in the case of Emerson, it was the Concord countryside, or with Fillmore, a farm in the American Midwest.

As to their views on Jesus, they stood together, startlingly enough, on something St. Augustine suggested more than 1,500 years ago in his revolutionary dictum: *That which is now called the Christian religion existed among the ancients, and never did it not exist from the beginning of the human race until Christ came in the flesh, at which time* the religion which already existed was called Christianity.

That was part of the seed and part of the thinking, and in the deepest of its meanings it meant Unity, unity with all people at all times and in all faiths; and America was now beginning to see the flowering of that seed in a new ministry.

I found that ministry expressed in impressive Unity churches during my research periods in the 1940-1960 years. In the heart of Kansas City in the Country Club Plaza stood Unity Temple, a million dollar structure opened for services on Easter day in 1950 and dedicated debt-free in 1960. In Los Angeles, New York, Detroit, Seattle, Santa Monica, Dallas, Houston, throughout Florida and the Midwest there were Unity churches, Unity centers. Almost every state had some kind of Unity activity. More than 100 churches were listed in 1941, 219 in 1964, and more than 300 in 1982.

Estimating the number of Unity worshipers was difficult because most centers were not stressing membership. The work was not that "churchified." The policy was to shy away from evangelization or proselytizing. There was never any mention of a denomination. Unity was a way of life no matter what your faith. Some Unity groups met on Sunday afternoons to avoid competing with the established churches and, wisely, to permit loyal church people who wanted extracurricular spiritual teachings to attend their churches and then drop around to Unity in the afternoon or evening. The Fillmore concept of Unity as a school was lodged in the consciousness of both center leaders and those who attended the centers. A loosely organized Unity Ministers Association had been formed in 1946 as if to guarantee integrity of the Fillmore principles and maintain a close relationship with Unity headquarters.

Center services, despite the fact that hymns were sung and a liturgical form of worship had developed, were generally unorthodox and non-traditional. The sermon was referred to as a lesson. Prayers were built on affirmations, the "inner light of Truth."

The service was not designed to "save the sinner" but to raise the consciousness, to experience healing, to recognize a oneness with God, to sense the joy of the Lord, to spell out methods for spiritual growth and an awareness of the Christ within. The joy of the Lord seemed to be getting through to people and they liked it. God, in Unity, wasn't averse to seeing His people smile in church or get a lift out of religion or exchange an embrace of fellowship. Jesus was presented as a Teacher who had a happier side to His nature than merely that of a *man of sorrows, and acquainted with grief.* (Isa. 53:3) There was a growing emphasis on youth work, Sunday schools, day schools, Youth of Unity activities. "Children," said Papa Charley, "were used by Jesus as an example of what we must become to enter the kingdom of the heavens. Most children are bubbling over with happiness." And that was true of most Unity adults. I once called it "the Unity glow."

Here was the Fillmore teaching gone public, taught and interpreted in a way that could be tested and tried in the world-at-large as it had been in the lives of Unity's co-founders and co-workers through their years of search and discovery. Here was Unity elbowing into Church Street, U.S.A.

But where did this burgeoning ministry suddenly come from?

Actually it wasn't so sudden. The seed of faith had been long in growing if you consider that it was planted even before there was a

Unity Farm. It went back to Tracy Avenue and earlier, back to the first Unity publication, back to the Society of Silent Help, to the lighted window.

It was as organic a growth in the religious field as any other religion that proved its worth. It reminded me of the history of Methodism. What John and Charles Wesley had in mind in 18th century England were Christian training centers, "Holy Clubs" where people of all faiths could experience what the Wesleys had encountered in the way of spiritual awakening. They had no intention of starting a church, but the *methodical discipline* of the Holy Club members led inevitably to a fellowship nicknamed by the public, "Methodists," and Methodism grew into an international multimillion-membered denomination that rocked the English church and took America by storm.

Unity began by training teachers. But when you train teachers in the spiritual field you are already training ministers. And when you begin training ministers, as was instituted when the Training School was officially established in 1930, you are sending out the call for those who feel the calling.

Where did the potential ministry come from? From everywhere. From people who read Unity literature, from study groups in private homes, from "Truth seekers" who took the correspondence courses, who caught the Fillmore charismatic fire, from people who had a healing, a vision, a wish, a curiosity, an awakening in the depth of their souls.

It was all part of the mystique. A God-centered movement, whether in oneself or in society, creates its own consciousness, draws its own plan, charts its own course, writes its own rules, and plays its own game. Then something does the sorting and the screening and reveals its own divine order in the fullness of time.

Unity, born in Truth and fostered in eclecticism, as Charles Fillmore openly admitted, "has taken Truth from many sources, for Truth is one and universal." Unity's awareness of the Christ within would, if one wished, be traceable to the early Christian mystics, whether in the "upper room" or wherever. Unity's emphasis on an inner light and a spiritual interpretation of the sacraments reminded me of Quakerism. Unity, like Christian Science, put major emphasis on spiritual steps to physical healing. Like Theosophy, it speculated about reincarnation and held it as a hypothesis worthy of consideration. Like Rosicrucianism, it contemplated the idea of cosmic reality and Spirit's all-embracing principles. Like traditional Christianity, it thought in terms of the art of deep and sincere worship. Awareness of the astral and psychic manifestations in life harked back to spiritualism. Hinduism's emphasis on meditation fit well into Unity's patterns for enlightenment. Home blessings, blessings of the mail, and prayers for protection had relationship to Jewish and Roman Catholic sources. Instead of a medal of Saint Christopher, patron saint of travelers in the Catholic faith, Unity had an affirmation to be put on the dashboard of your car:

GOD BLESS THIS AUTOMOBILE

This is God's car. God's hand is at the wheel. His wisdom chooses the way. God's law of order and right adjustment is manifest in all its mechanism. No fear alarms its occupants; for God's presence blesses them with the spirit of peace.

GOD BLESSES THE DRIVER OF THIS CAR

The driver of this car is an emissary of Spirit. God's wisdom inspires in

*him alertness, good judgment, and
quick decision. God's patience gives
him temperance and courtesy. The
Spirit of the Lord is upon him and
directs him in all his ways.*

It was not a single seed of faith that was
sown but seeds of many kinds. The Fillmores
insisted that no one church or philosophy had
a monopoly on Truth. Truth is immutable
law. Truth is God's absolutism. Truth is that
which is imminent and transcendent. Truth is
the realization that you are a child of God.

Is it any wonder that when this kind of
thinking is let loose on the planet things are
often at a risk? During these formative years
when Unity went public, such spiritual break-
throughs in thought and experience were
bound to attract people from every walk of
life, all sorts of people, a most wonderful mix,
from spiritual gypsies, as most of us are, to
philosophers of the Emersonian kind, as most
of us happen to be.

The tremendous idealism of Charles Fillmore, his irresistible faith in guidance, in
goodness and God, frequently permitted or
tempted students to take advantage of Unity
training and prompted them to set up their
own ambitious study groups under the Unity
name. Occasionally they went astray from

Unity's basic Truth principles.

Those embryonic days when Tracy was overrun with Unity enthusiasts, when the Unity Inn was serving meals for whatever the customer wished to pay, when vegetarianism was part of the discipline, and miracles were expected at every turn of the road were dramatic times indeed.

Don't forget Papa Charley's mother when you look back at the Tracy stage of the game, I told myself. She figured as strongly in the growth of the ministry as pioneer mothers did in the conquering of other American frontiers. For years she managed the Fillmore household while Charles and Myrtle were on lecture tours, attending classes, training teachers, writing books, and blessing the mail.

Many were the days when she was elbow deep in soapsuds, washing clothes or scrubbing pots and pans, and Charles would come along followed by a half-dozen bedraggled transients who had professed interest in things of the Spirit.

"Besides this," Charles would say, "they are hungry." And Myrtle would add, "They have a yearning for Truth."

Grandma Fillmore always served these wayfarers even though she may have been convinced that many of them had more of a yearning for a handout and a place to sleep. And Myrtle, quietly studying Charles, must often have thought, "God bless him. He is following his guidance." And so was Grandmother Fillmore following her guidance when, at suppertime, she would turn to Lowell or Rick and say, "Look down the street and see how many more they are bringing tonight."

Out of this humanism, this fabric of faith woven, at times, as some grand camouflage of God's secret design, came a vanguard of serious career-minded trainees who became the accredited teachers, way-showers of the expanding Unity way. That is where the ministry came from.

The candidates came from country towns and metropolitan centers, journeying to Kansas City and the miracles of Tracy Avenue and Unity Farm. They came to become what the Fillmores were, ministers of Truth. From the very beginning of the Unity movement there was a state of being called "consciousness." To those who experienced it, it was the spiral stairs, the upward climb of Spirit making its way through heart and mind into the awareness that there was something special God wanted them to do with their lives.

Women predominated in these formative years, largely because the metaphysical movement had no prejudices against female ministers. It presented an opportunity for spiritual expression and for careers in religious work. Here was a refreshingly unique unsexing and challenge to the ecclesiastical edict that had historically proclaimed, "There shall be only clergy*men* among the clergy."

Obviously, traditional churches failed to realize that Paul's admonition for women to "keep silence" in church had quietly gone by the board. Religion was in transition. The metaphysical movement was strongly "manned" by such modern-minded, gifted figures as Mary Baker Eddy, Emma Curtis Hopkins, Melinda Cramer, H. Emilie Cady, Ella Wheeler Wilcox, Ursula Gestfeld, and Myrtle Fillmore. It was consciousness that was at work, and Unity believed that God was at the heart of it.

In the early 1940s there were sixty ordained male Unity leaders and 115 female. In the early 1960s the ministerial roster consisted of 163 men and 312 women. In the 1980s, 312 women and 290 men. The Fillmores had been sparing in regard to ordination. Myrtle, particularly, was disinterested in degrees, honorary or earned, and was wary of titles. *Use the term 'Reverend' if you wish,* she once said, implying that it is allowable unless you begin to feel too proud about it, and added: *Charles and I do not have titles and do not judge people by their credentials.* Worthiness for ordination was based on spiritual, intellectual, and Christ-centered living fully as much as on completion of an academic study course.

Those who went into the field, men and women alike, and frequently husband and wife teams, usually carried no more than a teaching certificate and Charles Fillmore's blessing. To many this was "ordination" enough and sufficient accreditation for the calling they had experienced and the inspiration received by way of their studies.

There was, however, a legal factor. To perform marriages in most states, an ordination or a civil permit was a requisite. There were also social and professional requirements. To establish a church it was customary to be a member of the clergy. To be a minister for real and not just a "preacher" or an "evangelist," society demanded some kind of degree, even though, as a pundit once put it, "Jesus would have looked strange with a D.D. or a Ph.D. tacked to His name."

But times had changed since the disciples went about carrying *neither scrip, nor purse,* (Luke 10:4 A.V.) and when there were still lilies in the field and sheep in the meadow and not a car in sight. In our modern age, an ever more relevant Scripture text was *the laborer is worthy of his hire!* (Luke 10:7) And Unity's dedicated workers in the field were more than worthy.

Every center leader I talked to had his or her own story about the call to the Unity ministry. Many accounts are dramatic, and one is spectacular.

The center is Unity-by-the Sea. The place is Santa Monica, California. The founding minister is Sue Sikking. On Labor Day in 1939 a car accident left Sue, a young mother, with broken legs and a badly shattered jaw. She was in and out of surgery thirteen times while thirty pieces of broken bone were extracted or repaired. After seven months in a hospital bed she was told that she would never walk again and that she might conceivably die within ten days due to osteomyelitis threatening the brain.

"My first thought was to pray," she told me, "but I had never truly prayed before. I had simply repeated prayers. I was puzzled. I could not get down on my knees. I could not move in my bodycast. All I could do was to say from the bottom of my heart, God, if You will let me go home to my children, I will serve You the rest of my life. I turned over as best I could and tried to sleep. This was on a Wednesday night. I repeated my promise many times in the following days and during a long series of x-rays. On Monday the doctor said, 'I don't understand what is happening to your jaw. It has changed for the better; but I will say this, if it ever heals completely, it will be beyond anything we did here. There is nothing more we can do.' "

She went home several weeks later. The jaw had healed. She was able to walk with the aid of canes for a time, and eventually without them. A member of her family said to her, "That wasn't a prayer. You were trying to make a bargain with God."

Prayer or bargain, she remembered a little booklet called DAILY WORD that a friend had been sending to the Sikking family, but the booklet was rarely, if ever, read. Now, Sue, mother of five, went to Unity headquarters. Papa Charley became her special counselor, teacher, and personal friend. The time was the early forties. She was there when Lowell made public the discovery of Charles' and Myrtle's "Covenant." Sue had her own covenant with God and, with the beginning of Unity "teacher training," she came to Santa Monica and began a Unity work.

As she had learned to walk step-by-step on faith for physical healing, she now worked step-by-step on faith to build Unity-by-the-Sea and to inspire her husband and three of her five children to enter the Unity ministry. That, too, is how Unity grew!

Fully as important as the pastoral ministry expressed in the expanding centers was the ministry of the Word through headquarter's publications. The field ministry and the publishing department of Unity School were reciprocal. The center leaders and Unity literature were, so to say, "associate ministers." People went to a service and got interested in Unity writings. Receiving Unity writings through the mail they got interested in the center ministries. It worked both ways.

There were other important links in the chain of growth: The ever-phenomenal growth of Silent Unity; the publication and distribution through headquarters of inspirational books; radio programs sponsored by local centers with "Unity Viewpoint" material supplied by headquarter sources no less than by the field ministry. An expanding cassette department at the Village.

And here was a new TV program based on DAILY WORD, featuring Rosemary Fillmore Grace (now Rhea), daughter of Rick, who introduced special guests and celebrities on a five-minute coast-to-coast "thought for the day" presentation. Rosemary was Unity's first minister of the networks and "The Word" was heard and seen by a vast audience new to Unity and no doubt new to metaphysical teachings generally. Also coming in with a certain suddenness was Unity's "Dial-A-Prayer" telephone service, an open line in many Unity centers for anyone in need, a kind of Silent Unity action service with messages of hope and counsel.

Besides all of this there were now many loyal Protestants and a surprising sampling of Roman Catholics who were giving Unity literature a place next to their familiar denominational periodicals. In some homes the parish paper had been displaced by Unity material. Did ministers and priests object? Some did. Christian fundamentalists blasted Unity as atheistic and denounced it as a tool of the devil. They rated DAILY WORD as subtle propaganda for a Pollyanna type religion. They rejected, on the grounds of heresy, Unity's teaching that the Spirit of

God that dwelt in Jesus indwells every person, that the Virgin Birth could also be interpreted as the birth of Christ consciousness, that the origin of sin lies in humankind's ignorance, and that heaven and hell are not locations but states of consciousness. Some ministers, however, confessed that they were using the "Unity stuff" in their sermons and parish duties and that it produced profound results.

Typical of Protestant clerics who were "using the stuff" and who were to become Unity advocates was my close friend Dr. L. L. Dunnington, pastor of the prestigious First Methodist Church just off campus at the State University of Iowa in Iowa City. Tall, scholarly, outward-going, Lew was my companion on several research visits to Trappist monasteries, to Amish country, and excursions into spiritualistic camps at Chesterfield, Indiana, and Lily Dale, New York. He had an investigative mind and an adventurous flair that occasionally stretched his Methodist discipline. But it was elastic. A hardworking preacher, Lew was always on the hunt for usable ideas to supplement his effective ministry.

Dr. Dunnington's most productive and unforgettable trips were journeys with me to

Unity Farm in 1947 and again in 1948. He was, of course, impressed with the grounds, but his response to the people he met at Unity, their spirit and sense of dedication, went far beyond his expectations. He was fascinated by the youthful vigor of Papa Charley, entranced by Lowell's "commendable life-style," and thoroughly intrigued by Rick, all of whom gave him unlimited time and gifts of the Spirit by way of affection, openness about their life stories, and enough material for a season of sermons.

Lew told me on the way home (I was at the University of Iowa at the time) that the Unity Farm experience would change his ministry and his life. He was right. As far as his life was concerned, he willingly bore the brunt of both praise and defamation because of his "dabbling in the cults." As to his ministry, the attendance at his services increased from 400 to more than 2,000. His counseling proved more effective. Students were drawn to him. He introduced the use of Unity affirmation cards in his services. He put Unity prosperity techniques to work in his church and personal life. He stressed spiritual healing and authored a book, "Handles of Power," which was packed with ideas garnered from Unity and the New

Thought field. This book, published in 1952 under the Abingdon (Methodist) imprint, was so successful that Lew followed it up with a second Abingdon offering, adroitly titled, "More Handles of Power," and he fortified it with more Unity concepts.

That, too, was how Unity grew. There were other ministers of other denominations who, like Dr. Dunnington, introduced Unity principles and techniques in their parish work and found them productive. We shall meet some of them later. But it was now, during the 1940-1960 period, that the metaphysical movement in general and Unity in particular were in the exciting ferment of growth.

Did Fillmore recognize that, without some stronger organization out in the field and a more thoroughgoing ministerial training program at headquarters, the sowing of a new seed of faith in the public mind could logically be followed by a wild harvest for religious reapers? Was Unity itself a new thinker let loose on planet Earth?

Lowell Fillmore, assuming more and more responsibility in both administrative and educational functions, also saw the need for closer jurisdiction over Unity centers. Throughout the range of the metaphysical explosion many Unity ministers became innovators, testing their own theories and beginning to write their own books. But should there be as strong a hold on the teaching of Truth as was evidenced by Christian Science, for example, which made no apologies for being hierarchical in its structure and discipline? I knew from my own research of Christian Science that one had to dot every "i" and cross every "t" under the watchful mandate of Boston's Mother Church. Should Unity headquarters, being responsible for the training of its ministers, be equally jurisdictional? Clearly, that would be *unification* not *Unity.* Such a distinction could be understood, but what, I asked myself, is the difference between a spiritual fellowship, such as Unity, and so-called liberal Protestant denominations, such as Methodism, Congregationalism, or Unitarianism, as far as church government is concerned? On the other hand, is denominationalism really an offensive term, a dirty word? Couldn't there be an exercise of freedom and personal faith *within* a denominational framework?

I was to learn at firsthand the power of the Unity ministry in 1946 while teaching courses in contemporary religions at the State University of Iowa. The inclusion of accredited courses in religion at a state university, despite the separation of church and state, was itself innovative. Inviting guests from non-traditional religious movements was even more exciting. I introduced my students to a wide range of spiritual leaders from Amish to Zoroastrians, and I had as my guest in November of 1946 L. E. Meyer, minister of Unity Temple in Kansas City.

I had met L. E. previously when visiting Unity Village with Dr. Dunnington. I had the endorsement of my administrative boss, Dr. M. Willard Lampe, at the university, the blessings of Lowell Fillmore, and the generous acceptance of L. E. to have him discuss the Unity movement with my class of some 200 students. This was to be followed by an unrestricted talk-back on Unity's beliefs and practices.

L. E., gracious, scholarly, quiet spoken, radiating Unity confidence and Unity calm, made a remarkable impression on both students and an enthusiastic Midwestern radio audience who tuned in regularly to this course, broadcast over Station WSUI. The response left no question about Unity's contemporary appeal. It spoke in the idiom of our time. It addressed itself to one's personal needs. It was both simple and profound. Its teachings covered a reach of mind from Christian liberals to non-churched and non-Christian seekers alike. It was sufficiently Christ-centered and eclectic to address itself to our interfaith campus gathering.

Judging by the prolonged question-answer period following the class session, interest in metaphysical thought and Rev. Meyer's ministry ran high. It also cut straight across the registered students' roll, which included many facets, from GIs who had signed up for the course because of a genuine search, to liberal arts students who had enrolled for little more reason than picking up a few academic credits.

L. E.'s visits with special guests and an evening with faculty members and representatives of the local clergy were also all to the good as far as interspiritual and intercultural relations were concerned.

Based on the "fan mail" that came in to WSUI, it would seem that every request for more information about Unity could represent the potential of a Unity study group in the Midwest, just as we may assume that every person who inquired about getting into the Unity ministry would represent another Unity center somewhere in God's good time.

I wrote to Lowell Fillmore, expressing my delight with L. E.'s presence and presentation. Lowell replied with a characteristically confident note that everything was in divine order and that the work was continually growing according to God's plan, as had always been the case.

When I asked myself again whether Unity was becoming another denomination, I answered my question with another, "Does it really matter?" Or was it one already? And Rick's classic line came back to me, "Talk to Lowell or Father about that."

Why not talk to Papa Charley? He and Cora spent a good deal of their time on the West Coast. They had a home in the Los Angeles area where they pursued their writing careers and occasionally toured the ministerial field. I planned to meet them in 1948 during my West Coast research of the Self Realization movement and an appointment with its founder, Paramahansa Yogananda, at his Mt. Washington (Los Angeles) estate.

While on this assignment, I learned that Papa Charley, now nearing his 94th year, had cancelled some of his trips and returned to Unity Village. I was sorry to have missed him, but learned that while he was visiting at Unity-by-the-Sea in Santa Monica, he mentioned to Sue Sikking that he was not feeling well, and confessed, "I'll be glad to get back home." Cora, always solicitous, always in attendance, always so mindful of Papa Charley's greatness that she constantly referred to him respectfully as "Mr. Fillmore," quickly decided they should return to the Farm.

Perhaps Cora was more concerned than he because his indomitable will to live once prompted him to state publicly that he might never die, at least that was the impression that was given. *My body is constantly renewing itself cell by cell,* he avowed, and added: *There is no reason why life cannot be constantly extended.* He was a born immortalist.

But now, everyone had Papa Charley very much in mind. He was not one to cancel an appointment unnecessarily. Interestingly enough, it would soon be June Conference time at headquarters and this year, 1948, would see more ordinations than ever before. The entire get-together was slated to be especially significant. Among other things, Unity Temple, under the leadership of L. E. Meyer, was to be officially opened to the public on June 29. Unity was calling it the culmination of "Years of Fulfillment."

I had attended the Conference and Training School program two years earlier and shared in activities that continued from May to October. At that time the training sessions were organized on a four-term basis with six weeks to a term. During my stay I realized the power of the love and adoration bestowed on this almost legendary figure, the much loved Papa Charley. I felt this affection whenever I met representatives of Unity's past, present, and future. The teaching staff consisted of men and women steeped in the tradition and joy of the movement. Ernest C. Wilson, illustrious minister of Christ Church Unity, Los Angeles, conducted a course, "Preparation and Preservation of Unity Lectures." A dedicated East Coast colleague, Georgiana Tree West of New York, lectured in the same course during a later term. Here was another great name in Unity. The leader of South Side Unity Center in Kansas City, Ida Palmer, taught "Spiritual Healing." Francis G. Gable, editor of *Good Business*, conducted a seminar called "Spiritual Clinic," and lectured on "Human Relations." Charles' and Cora's names appeared together on the staff of the Training School. Cora's spirit, refinement, and dedication to Unity's principles qualified her as a teacher no less than as the devoted wife of Charles.

The student body, preponderantly women, consisted for the most part of those preparing themselves for the ministry. Requirements for ordination were the completion of the correspondence course, a methods-and-ideas course, two terms at the Training School, and one year of work at a center. There was also a liberal sprinkling of men and women who came solely for self-improvement. Mingling with them, I saw in this phase of the training an attractive spiritualized course in how to win friends and influence people, how to be healthy, wealthy, wise, and spiritually integrated. A number of Protestant ministers were also on board in the hope of weaving more of Unity's strands into their own denominational fabric.

At Conference time the accolades and interest were generously distributed, but they centered magnetically on one man, Charles Fillmore. Here, as in his classes, his natural abilities reinforced by experience and an exalted faith reached out in auric fashion to touch his listeners. Here Papa Charley was at his best. "Fundamentals of Unity Principles," "Prosperity," and "How to Apply God to Everyday Living" were some of his teaching titles. But the major course at Conference was the man himself.

He was watched and revered wherever he went. Devotees persistently sought him out.

"How are you getting along on your latest book, Mr. Fillmore?" "Papa Charley, they tell me you are going on another tour." "You're looking wonderful, sir!" "How is the Training School work going in Los Angeles?" "Do you like the West Coast?" "Your assembly message was worth the trip!" "Mr. Fillmore, when will you come to our center? Everyone is expecting you!"

Sensitive to every question, he listened patiently, quietly studying the face of the speaker, as I recalled he studied me in our first meeting on Tracy. Now, at this Conference, I knew him and he knew me. It was here I asked him frankly, "Is Unity becoming a denomination?" And he said to me, "Unity is a school of Christianity. As such it is an independent educational institution. All of our centers are places of religious research for all. We have no creed, but we are eager to serve the people of every creed."

I didn't know that this would be the last time I would see him. I was to remember him as he was that day, his hand resting upon the arm of Cora; his eyes seeing visions beyond my knowing.

Sometimes, lost in a spiritual hiatus, he seemed to retreat into the hopeful shadows of his ninety-odd years. Startlingly free of the marks of age, here was a spiritual pioneer who had deliberately worked at the business of staying young. Even his thinning white hair did not add age. His language was couched in the phrases that had made his books basic texts in the Unity world: *The superconsciousness of Christ in man has mastery and dominion over all conditions of mind and body. Jesus was the result of a series of incarnations. In the person of Jesus of Nazareth is manifested the highest state of consciousness. His superconsciousness was His real self, and through it He was able to redeem His body. In like manner, when we learn the process, we can transform and redeem our bodies and take on Christ-consciousness. This age is ready for it and there are men and women among us who can achieve these things.*

I had the feeling, born out of my studies and whatever else adds weight to one's convictions, that certain spiritual leaders who live their lives closely to the Giver of life are invariably endowed with a spiritual second sight about the closing phases of their earthly stay. This was true about the passing of Myrtle Fillmore on October 6, 1931. She unpretentiously made quiet preparations for her transition several weeks before her passing.

She told a young Silent Unity worker, who years later told me, that as she was blessing the mail one day, a voice said to her, "God wants you to bless the mail from the next plane of life. You will be able to accomplish much more that way." Myrtle confided to several other workers in Silent Unity, "I want to be used by God, for His highest good and mine." Until the very day of her departure she was active, walking about, conversing as one preparing for nothing more than an appointment with a cherished friend.

And so I pictured Papa Charley suddenly returning to Unity Village from California, guarded and guided by Cora. I imagined he must have had thoughts of Myrtle's valor close in mind as now, for the first time in his God-given ninety and more years, he asked someone to take his place in conferring the ordinations at Conference time. He selected L. E. Meyer to be his stand-in on this occasion. I surmise he must have remembered how Myrtle stood with him on the platform three nights before her transition and how active and resigned she was until the very moment of her foreshadowed passing. There must have passed through his mind the fortitude with which both he and Myrtle accepted as inevitable the death of their beloved Royal, their third son, in 1923. And how a Unity minister once said of Myrtle's dying, "She left the world only because she willed to go."

He must have remembered how gently his mother, Grandma Fillmore, took her flight at ninety-seven, in March 1931, and how Myrtle referred to the passing of her treasured mother-in-law as one *who slipped from sight and touch of the sense consciousness only, for we know that in omnipresent love there can be no separation.*

Such premonitions have happened to many people at many times. From legendary spiritual figures to Jesus, from orthodox believers to self-styled freethinkers who often have God very close in heart. Those who live near the source of light have eyes to see the commonly unseen.

And that is why I believe that, when Charles Fillmore came to the inevitable moment, which has spared no one as far as we know, and which is as much a part of life as life itself, he did say to Lowell and to Cora who were with him on the night of July 4th, a Sunday night, "Don't you see it? Don't you see it?" And he gazed upward and whispered, entranced, "The new Jerusalem coming down from God, the new heaven and the new earth!

Don't you see it?"

He left his earthly body the following morning, July 5, 1948 at ten o'clock. The news spread quietly and quickly from Unity Village to Unity Temple and into the field of ministry wherever the new seeds of faith had been sown and where a new church was being born, a church with truths that contain shallows in which a child can wade and depths in which a giant must swim.

Part Two

Patterns for the Present

(1960s—1980s)

Chapter I

The Unity Viewpoint

A Sunday morning is many things—a time for sleep or a time for play, a time for work or breakfast in bed, a time for the Sunday edition or waking to the music from a campanile, as I did on this Sunday morning at Unity Village.

The song was decidedly orthodox: *The morning light is breaking, the darkness disappears* . . . It was also a reminder that breakfast would soon be served in the Inn, and that seven o'clock might be a good time for getting up.

My motel room was Number One, the first of twenty identical rooms in one long unit. West across the spacious court were clusters of cozy cottages. These accommodations, within easy walking distance of the main headquarters buildings, were comfortable, quiet, air-conditioned quarters for visitors and people on spiritual retreats. Some of the cottages also served as residences for Unity workers.

Here on my little motel desk was a copy of

131

DAILY WORD, never failing in its persuasive affirmations that God's in His heaven and all's right with the world, despite the fact that the 1960s were upon us with clouds of world unrest and racial strife.

DAILY WORD proclaimed on this particular Sabbath morning: *I am one with God.*

I am One with God's Light; I am One with His Life. I am One with His Love; I am One with His Good. To be One with Him, I must Unify Myself with Him in prayer.

I must turn quietly within, where I can shut out all thought of the outer world, all that has disturbed my tranquillity and peace.

How right, how true, how typically Unity. It lost no time in assuring the reader of an intimate consciousness of God, full and complete. It begged no question and raised no hint of doubt. It said nothing about the need for penance or self-renunciation before God could be approached or His presence utilized. It made no reference to inborn sin or evil or Satan at work in the world. It simply and confidently affirmed:

As I feel my Oneness with God in prayer, He strengthens my faith and fills me with

*courage. As I lift my mind and heart to Him I
am Guided and helped.*

*I find strength and the faith to meet life
courageously, for I am drawing upon the
Mighty, Unlimited Source of Power, of Peace,
of Love.*

*I am One with God Whose Love Enfolds
All Creation.*

That was my beginning for a Unity day, a
customary beginning for every Unity day
because each reading in DAILY WORD,
though it differs from the others in content, is
quarried out of the same inexhaustible mine
of faith and on the same indomitable assurance that God is in us and we are in God.

Since my introduction to DAILY WORD
during the Tracy research days, I had run
across scores of people who read it and lived
by it—Catholics, Protestants, Jews, Bud-
hists, Moslems, churched and unchurched
people. A gift subscription had been given to
me by a Roman Catholic woman from Ceylon.
Whenever I read this daily capsule for spiritual living, I felt in the company of people of
all faiths and cultures; and here at Unity
Village this *entente spirituale* took on an

especially deep and personal thrust. Remembrances of Unity and its kindness to me came back with new meaning. Just now, as far as world conditions were concerned, I told myself that one cannot correct corrupt conditions until one is strong enough not to be corrupted by the conditions one wishes to correct. Metaphysical religions, and Unity in particular, were reminding us that religion is first and foremost an inside job.

When I started along the winding road that led from the motel to the Inn, I had the feeling that other visitors who walked the grounds had found their Sunday orientation at the same source as I. They, too, were conceivably turning over in their minds the reminder that *I am one with God,* and very likely thinking the thoughts that I was, thinking them with me—in unity. Why do we so often forget our Oneness and feel alone and adrift in a universe which God has made and which, somehow, He will most certainly control no matter how foolhardy we may be? Were they as fascinated, I wondered, at the realization of how quickly one's attitude toward life changes when we have the courage to recognize this Oneness?

DAILY WORD had planted the seed, *I am one with God,* and the Unity grounds were nourishing it, grounds that on this particular morning were like a quiet college campus or a place inside protecting walls, though how well I knew there were no walls and nothing monastic about Unity Village!

There are no special disciplines invoked here, and there is certainly nothing superciliously religious about those who tarry here for spiritual input. What Unity is interested in is the discovery of the indwelling Spirit, and that Spirit is inescapable when you hold to the Word: *I am one with God.*

Since the days of Papa Charley, my work had taken me to the headquarters of many religious movements around the world, and they all had their individuality and existed by the very right of their existence. On my own, on State Department assignments through its Cultural Affairs Department, and on special missions, I had lived and worshiped with people of many religious persuasions and cultural expressions. From Sarnath in India, where Buddhism began, to the Holy Land, where Christianity was born; from the Vatican, stronghold of Roman Catholicism, to Protestant fortresses at Wittenberg and Geneva; from the fountainhead of the Baha'i faith on Mt. Carmel in Israel, to the gigantic halls of Rissho Koseikai in Japan; in each and all, in some special way God had imparted a certain interpretation of his will for humankind.

I felt this overpoweringly on this Sunday morning while the music from the campanile cast its Sabbath spell on all of us. The tower and the Silent Unity lighted window brought back special thoughts of Rick and Lowell, and I looked forward to seeing them again during this stay. There was evidence of new structures being built and things being repaired, but the red-tiled roofs atop the stately buildings, the immaculately tended hedges, the magnificent elms and maples and rows of ash, blending into a warmth of color, augmented the Sunday mood. In a series of archways of the Silent Unity building, the Cloisters, there was nothing hidden or mysterious. Romantically, you had a feeling that Unity had no dark passages, no forbidden doors, no restricted areas, not even a sign cautioning you to stay off the grass or "Please don't pick the roses." You were on your own.

Just now Unity was not really a village or a movement or a creed or a headquarters, it was a feeling, a relaxed and confident feeling that: *I am one with God—and God is good.*

Whether you idealize religion or whether

you are completely cold-blooded about its function in mortal life, on a Sunday morning at Unity you neither want nor need a theology more profoundly simple than the feeling of a nearness to a Oneness.

My thesis had long been that "all roads that lead to God are good." Each great religion stands before us as a specific path to spiritual consciousness, to the *I am one with God* awareness expressed in DAILY WORD.

Among the great religions of the world, Zoroastrianism is the path of righteousness; Judaism the path of the law; Hinduism the path of identification; Buddhism the path of deliverance; Confucianism the path of harmony; Islam the path of submission; Humanism the path of reason; Shintoism the path of the Kami; Christianity the path of love. Unity, a synthesis of religions distilled in the essence of Christianity, is essentially the path of goodness. It says *God is good* and never ceases affirming it.

Charles Fillmore, though he was never completely free of physical disability, contended that the goodness of God makes every thought to the contrary an illusion. In simple faith he insisted that, "God made all people good and all good people nice." He kept on assuring himself of this, and out of this viewpoint came Unity's most forceful affirmation and favorite invocation: *There is but one Presence and one Power in the universe, God the Good Omnipotent.*

Unity followers are challenged to follow this axiom all the way, wherever the way may lead. They are urged not only to say, "There is one Presence and one Power in the universe," but they add, "in my life," and "in the world," and "in my experiences," "in my affairs," "in my business," one Presence and one Power, God the Good Omnipotent!

Thinking about this, I stood for a moment on the flower-scented grounds and asked myself, "How sincerely do you believe this 'one Presence and one Power' declaration? Set the phrase against your church's teachings and your honest convictions, and what are you going to do with it? Say you have a problem so critical that it simply *must* turn out as you insist. You pray about it. You put it into God's hands, so to say. You are even willing, hesitantly though it may be, to declare divine order no matter what. Will you still say that God is good? Will you still truthfully affirm that: *There is one Presence and one Power in my life, God the Good Omnipotent* if your problem continues to be a problem and there is no solution and things don't work out the way you think they should? Do Unity people actually follow through on this? Do Unity people really believe it?" And something stubbornly said to me, "The point is not what Unity people believe, what do *you* believe? Which way are *you* willing to go?"

My dialogue continued. "Say that you are sick. Say that you have a seemingly incurable disease. What then? Say that something suddenly tragic comes your way. Then what about the Unity viewpoint that God is good? Can you as an intelligent and realistic person really look at the world-at-large and subscribe to this philosophy? Can rational beings conscientiously repeat these affirmations in the light of their lives from which evil and suffering and sickness and death are never more than a step away? Come on, analyze your life and then honestly decide whether there is but one Presence and one Power, God the Good Omnipotent!"

Suddenly I realized it was a hazy morning. Objective creature that I am, I try to see all sides of an equation. In spite of my research or, perhaps because of it, I shied away from an absolute like a wild horse shies from a glaring light, or, even worse, I was as afraid of running blindly into an irrational belief as the same horse would rush blindly into a fire. Just now it seemed to me that Unity was all too uncritical, all too unrealistic, all too naive in its point of view. It dawned on me, as it often had in other religions and in other cultures, that it is easy to lose a rational perspective on the big world when you find a microcosm of quiet and peace at the head-quarters of the faithful. Had I romanticized Unity too much in my early, intimate re-search?

It is easy to say that hunger and sickness, suffering and inhumanity, injustice and war are mere illusions when you are well fed and secure, and when your little world is pleasant and compact. But if God is not *consistently* good, how good is He? Who is to say, "He is good in this instance but not in that"? If we believe He is all good, why do we ever com-plain or fear or lose hope? On the other hand, what kind of a mind is it which, when we ask of it, "What if God is not good?" simply answers, "But He is! How can He be other-wise?" And that was an answer I usually got from Unity followers.

Then, to be ultra-honest, I admitted to myself that the reason these questions bugged me now was that I did have a prob-lem that had been confronting me for some time. I secretly felt that if I came to Unity again, as I was doing, some solution might be forthcoming. In fact, I had half a notion to talk to Lowell Fillmore about it if the chance presented itself without too much embarrassment to me!

I decided I needed some breakfast. Perhaps a man shouldn't wrestle with these problems on an empty stomach. There are religions like Catholicism, for example, in which you partake of the Eucharist before eating, and after the Eucharist you do not feel like arguing about God. You simply believe. Something has been proved to you, though you may not be able to logically explain the process. You walk away from the communion with hands touching in prayer, *believing.* Like Papa Charley who with childlike faith never ceased to proclaim that "God is good, you wait and see," you walk away from the Eucharist-of-the-mind through a world of your own. Or, rather, through God's world. You walk away and in that moment, no matter what your trial or struggle may have been, the haze lifts and you know beyond a doubt that God is good.

So I made my way to the heavily carved walnut doors, the doors Rick had built, to the entrance of Unity Inn. No sooner had I entered than I heard someone call my name. Greeting me was a young, enthusiastic Unity minister who had come to the Village for a conference. He was one of a group of a hundred or so men and women who were chatting away in this spacious dining hall and moving through the cafeteria line, all in happy moods, while a man at a piano quietly and casually played a hymn: *Safely through another week, God has brought us on our way.* In the spirit of the song, the minister and I selected our eggs and toast and fruit and drink and carried our trays to one of the highly polished tables. Here we ate and talked about many things, but we both knew what was going through the other's mind, memories of our previous get-together.

The last time I had met this Unity friend was when I spoke at his magnificent center in West Palm Beach, Florida, a church built and served by the effective co-ministry of this man and his wife. A short week before Mrs. Bach and I arrived at their church, this couple had lost their youngest child, a boy of eighteen months, in a drowning tragedy in the swimming pool of their new home.

They had left the child in the care of a young woman while they went about some church duties. In an unguarded moment the child wandered off and slipped into the pool. When the frantic woman spied the boy in the water, she jumped in though unable to swim, and, after futilely trying to save the youngster, ran hysterically to a neighbor's home for help.

By the time the parents were notified, the boy had been rushed to the hospital where all efforts to revive him had failed. My wife and I arrived, as I have said, about a week after this happened. We knew how dearly the boy had been loved and how intense the sorrow of the parents must have been. But we were to learn that in all of our intimate experiences and participation in suffering among the children of men, we had never seen such a demonstration of fortitude and faith as that evidenced by these Unity-trained leaders. I was sure I would never forget how, the very day after the drowning, the father led his three other children into the pool and here, standing in the water, they reaffirmed their faith and reestablished their confidence that life should hold no fear, that everything is ever in divine order and that God is good. I have seen evidences of faith before, but such a declaration I had not seen. It was Unity at work at the nerve center of life, and to me it was a way of wonder.

Our stay with them turned out to be one of our most faith-filled weeks. Now, once more, at the breakfast table in the cafeteria at Unity Village, I recalled the unconquerable confidence of the boy's mother. I remembered that during the moments that the doctors were trying to invoke life back into the tiny body of her son, she was in a hospital waiting room praying her affirmative prayers. Unity does not implore God. It does not plead with God. It does not even petition God. Unity simply affirms that God's will is done and that that will is good.

That was how this mother prayed, and during her prayer, she spied a copy of Unity's DAILY WORD. That a copy should have been in the hospital room is not unusual, but it happened that this was not a current issue but one that bore the exact month and year of her son's birth. What was more, it contained a poem devoted to the passing of a child, and it spoke of God's great love unfolding through the circumstance.

The mother was as impressed by this as if God had placed the copy there with His own hand. As far as she was concerned, He *had* placed it there. The father of the boy, sitting with me at the cafeteria table, said, "Some people would say these things are just coincidental, but when we say that, what have we said? Since everything is in God's hands, isn't that in God's hand, too? Some people ask me how I can bear to look at the pool, remembering all that happened. It wasn't the pool that did it. The pool is what you believe it to be in your consciousness. I look at it as if it were the biblical pool where an angel came down and stirred the waters, the waters of life, and filled them with healing. I know that I will now be better able to help and heal others who go through similar experiences. If faith does not meet these needs, of what good is faith?"

As we talked, I thought of my strictly orthodox mother, a Christian of the old school, deeply, sincerely, devoutly committed to the doctrines of the German Reformed Church. I could not help but contrast her attitude about tragedies and death with that of this typical Unity leader. Mother interpreted a drowning or any kind of sudden death as the whiplash of an angered God. We never had a death among our relatives without my mother suggesting that they sell the house and move out. When we had a passing in our family, the rooms were thoroughly fumigated, as much to remove the curse of death as for any hygienic reason, and once, after the premature demise of my only sister, we actually did sell the big house to appease, it seemed to me, the wrath of a chastising God.

These Unity parents, however, wished only to bless their home anew, as they had blessed the pool. They saw not the scourge of God, but an angel moving on the water. They took what could have been a fateful blow and used it to deepen their convictions that God is good. They had an affirmation: *There is one Presence and one Power in the universe, God the Good Omnipotent.*

As I thought about all this on this Sabbath morning here in the cafeteria at Unity Village, I concluded that mortal man has at least two choices: my mother's which represented the approach of old-time Christianity, and my long ago church on Wabash, or the choice of these young Unity leaders who typified Unity's insistence that all things work together for good.

They really typified it. They accepted the circumstances surrounding the death of their child as precious fragments which, when pieced together, would be restored once more into the perfect image of God's good will.

It is truly quite a point of view, this Unity viewpoint that I was always seeing through new eyes. Evidently, when you live and move in this consciousness of God's goodness, there is no doubt as to how far you will go in trusting in divine omnipotence. You go all the way. You do not say, "I believe up to this point." You never exclaim, "Here I must abandon my faith." Since God's will is sovereign in the universe, you *know* that His will enfolds *everything*. Since He is good, He is *all* good. If you do not fully understand a circumstance or a situation, you nonetheless believe and trust that God never ordains disorder, never sees us as anything less than His creation, and never had any other end in mind than that of causing us in the long run to realize our eternal potential of oneness with Him.

That is what the Unity minister was telling me. He was making it clear that it did not just *happen* that a fellow minister was in Palm Beach in time to conduct the memorial service for his son. It was no *accident* that the distraught housekeeper now found a new meaning in religion. It was not just *coincidence* that my wife and I came to their home when we did. All of these occurrences were part of divine order, evidences of the goodness of God in which there is always meaning and which is everlastingly alive with purpose.

Purpose. Unity believes that there is always purpose.

Meaning. Unity believes that nothing happens without meaning.

Divine Order. Unity affirms that every intricate detail of life is bound by the omnipotence of God.

Unity insists that all life is one and that everything in life is related to everything else. There is a line, a chain of circumstance, a continuity, and in it all things work together for good. Unity believes that chance is God at work, that a hunch is the whispering of Divinity, that what we call fate is cosmic purpose, and that coincidence is immutable law. Live with a horizon that knows no ending! Get the vastness of infinite vision! Life is an adventure in faith!

What a way to live, if one has the will to believe!

And how does one develop the will? One way may be to mingle with Unity people. If you wish to excel in music, meet and hear the best musicians; if you wish to be an artist, study the best art; if you wish to learn spiritual techniques, observe and mingle with those who have employed these techniques in their lives.

That is how it seemed to me as breakfasters

came and went and as I was surrounded by those who knew me and who were quite ready to join in the conversation whatever the topic might be. After all these intervening years, I realized all over again that Unity people are friendly people. You can recognize them by what I once half seriously called "the Unity glow." It was my attempt to describe a certain radiance typical of those who somehow are persuaded in their souls that God is good; and I say this with no intention of implying that Unity people are either saintly or beatific or that they are necessarily better than people in any other faith!

By and large, however, I became more and more convinced that they are individuals who have found something to live by and who have made the living of it an adventure. They seem to have a good time believing. They give the impression that there are at least two things which a God of goodness is opposed to: self-righteousness and morbidity. They believe in the therapy of the happy heart and in the reminder that what is beautiful is good and that whatever is good is also beautiful.

They represent practically all major religious backgrounds, and it is safe to say that they came to Unity seeking something which their traditional faith had not supplied—physical healing, escape from a God of wrath, the need for a positive, hopeful, spiritual environment, a search for the common unity of all religions, the challenge of faith in action. No doubt many came as a secret revolt against the institutionalized church which seemingly had lost the personal touch. But most of all, they came because they wanted to believe with all their heart that God is good.

As I listened to the conversation and reflected on the minister's attitude about the son he had lost—but did not lose—my problem suddenly seemed of very little consequence, and I was about ready to turn it over to God, too, and let it go at that.

Most of us would like to do this, but we lack the courage. We lack the glory of the "foolhardy faith" which, when it has done the best it can, assures us that God is somehow working out His will in our behalf. Most of us readily profess that God is good, but we do not live as though the profession were true. We have the phrase but not the faith. Most of us pretend that our religion makes us happy, but it doesn't. The majority of us claim that we trust God, but we don't. We have our reservations and our disclaimers and our secret conviction that He cannot quite be trusted, perhaps because of our secret sense of guilt that we have not measured up to this trust.

Thinking through all of this, I gradually realized that the piano music had stopped, that the campanile was quiet, and that suddenly there was one of those moments when the voices in the cafeteria were hushed and the whole world seemed still. My father once told me that these moments usually happen at twenty minutes after the hour or at twenty minutes to. He said it was the time when the angels held their breath. I have no idea where this superstition originated or what this cosmic hiatus is all about, but often during such times I glance at my watch. I did so now. It was twenty minutes after nine. Breaking the quiet with a laugh, I said, "If a person could just hold on to his childlike faith . . . "

"As for instance?" someone inquired.

"As for instance the feeling that God is consistently good," I said.

To which a woman at the table responded, "But He is consistently good! How could He be otherwise?"

Lowell Fillmore had come into the room without pretense, as he would have to, for there was never the slightest affectation about him. In fact, I was sure that I had changed considerably more than he in appearance and temperament since our previous meeting years ago. No one would ever call him the majordomo of the Unity household, yet that, in a very real way, was where he stood as far as the coordinator of the spiritual and physical functions of the movement were concerned. He would rather say that Unity has but one director, the heavenly Father, one general manager, Jesus Christ, and one trouble shooter, the Holy Spirit. It also has just one basic tenet: God is good, and one invocation: *There is one Presence and one Power in the universe, God the Good Omnipotent.*

"Don't get up, don't get up," he said when I rose to greet him. He added with a chuckle, "The Sabbath was made for rest."

Very little had changed with Lowell. Unity may have changed around him, but he was the unmoved mover of the movement. I recalled my first visit at Tracy when I asked, "Where do I find Lowell Fillmore?" And the reply was, "He's here," or "He's over there," or "He's at his desk. Go and talk to him."

Since Papa Charley's passing, Lowell had dedicated Unity centers all over the western hemisphere. He had written innumerable articles and was carrying on a correspondence with the great and near great among America's figures in many walks of life. He had spoken to capacity audiences and presided over scores of Unity meetings, conferences, and retreats. But he wanted to be nothing more than a Unity worker, desiring very little, envying no one, residing with his wife Alice in a house that Rick built, living in a world of such remarkable tranquillity that others were automatically calmed by his presence. Whatever doubts may have beset him, he had hidden them perfectly. Whatever problems he may have had, he made them indiscernible. Whatever disquietude he may have suffered, he never let anyone see any other token of his faith except that God is good.

We had only a few moments before the Sunday school period in the chapel, but it wasn't the pressure of time that kept me from talking to Lowell about my problem, it was the momentary paradox of feeling that the problem did not exist. In fact, when I skirted the very edge of my concern and felt him out, so to say, he switched the subject and told me about a set of books he wanted to give me dealing with the lost continent of Mu. Did I know that the Garden of Eden might possi-

153

bly have been part of a new sunken island in the mid-Pacific and that Easter Island might be a fragment of this lost continent?

"I hear you have been to Angkor in Cambodia," he said. "Well, you know the civilization of Angkor that mysteriously disappeared? That may be part of the whole great story of how the idea of God traveled from Mu to Angkor to Egypt and all around. Think of the thousands of years and the civilizations that have come and gone and people are still searching, still searching today. It is really wonderful."

It was equally wonderful how quickly he had got me to think in terms of endless time and forgotten cultures when I had a personal problem that I thought had to be solved immediately!

The things that seemed vital to others seemed of small importance to Lowell unless God was first involved in the story. And when God was involved, the perplexities were automatically dissolved.

"What would you say," I asked him point blank, "if a person had a problem and, praying and thinking and struggling with it for more than a month, he found absolutely no solution?"

"In a case like this," he said reflectively,

"it could be that the person has been trying too hard. There are things we cannot do by ourselves, but when we just quietly turn them over to God, He does them easily."

He looked at me as if to say, "But you probably know that as well as I."

"By the way," he said, "are you going over to the first service, the Sunday school? We can walk together if you like."

That is what we did. We went from the cafeteria through the printing plant quarters where the presses stood hushed in Sabbath silence, and took the elevator to the chapel where people were gathering for this quiet, informal session.

As I sat with Lowell in the unpretentious surroundings made beautiful by the consciousness that God is good, I thought of a poem that this unassuming man at my side had written and titled "The Answer":

When for a purpose
I had prayed and prayed and prayed
Until my words seemed worn and bare
*   With arduous use,*
And I had knocked and asked and
*   knocked and asked again,*
And all my fervor and persistence
Brought no hope,
I paused to give my weary brain a rest

And ceased my anxious human cry.
In that still moment,
After self had tried and failed,
There came a glorious vision of God's power,
And, lo, my prayer was answered in that hour.

The session began. The leader asked us to stand and join in an invocation. He recited it and we then repeated it together: *There is one Presence and one Power in the universe, God the Good Omnipotent.*

After this we remained for a time in silence, letting the words sink into consciousness until they became absolute Truth, from which there is no willing escape, and in which there should be only hope and joy.

We then sat down while the soloist sang "The Lord's Prayer," an ever beautiful number which prepared us for the meditation. These are the moments in Unity when the world becomes still and relaxed and one experiences the presence of God in a special way. Then the leader said, "You know, God always makes the right decisions in our lives. Until He says, 'Go,' don't go. He will make it clear and you will know."

It was an uncanny moment. It was as if the leader had read my thoughts and answered my question. My particular problem had to do with leaving my university post and pulling up the roots of some eighteen years. To me it was a big decision with many overtones and implications, and I had been putting it off with characteristic procrastination. I had *prayed and prayed,* and now, when for a moment *I paused to give my weary brain a rest,* the minister's words came as a positive direction. For God had surely never said "Go!" to me in a voice plain enough for me to hear! But now I did seem to hear Him say that I should *not* go just yet, and it all seemed right and true to me.

Lowell sat quietly with his hands in his lap. What he or others felt I did not know, but for me just then it was more than the beginning of just another Sunday. It was "The Answer." The morning had been more than a reading of DAILY WORD and a meeting with Unity friends. It was already something of a Eucharist in which one wished to linger and, finding his problem mysteriously and wondrously solved, live more confidently in the belief that God is good.

I needed no persuasion when Lowell whispered that we hold our seats for the church service which was to follow and for which the worshipers were already beginning to assemble.

Chapter II

How Unity Worships

A Unity service is so subtle in its simplicity that newcomers will either be profoundly impressed or completely bewildered, depending on their points of view.

I was convinced of this again as I sat among the worshipers at the service in Unity Village Chapel. Here we were in a sprawling room filled to overflowing with some 600 men and women, and having very little architecturally to suggest a traditional church-like atmosphere. There was a lectern in the center of the semicircular, red-carpeted platform; the organist at the console and the woman soloist were attired in choir robes, but there the formality ended. The young minister wore a business suit. No altar or cross adorned this serviceable sanctuary. No candles burned and no statues or stained glass windows suggested anything ecclesiastical. But what one *felt* was a sense of worship, and perhaps true religion is first of all a feeling, a comfortable feeling, bringing God down to where we live and us up to where God resides, only that in Unity there is no up and down to God's "isness." Seeing is believing, but feeling is knowing; and just now we had the feeling.

The secret of a Unity service is instantly revealed in the affirmation, an affirmative pronouncement carefully, almost delicately placed in a contemplative setting. Go to any Unity church and before the service is five minutes old, you have participated in corporate worship. Something has happened to you. You have professed with your lips and confessed with your heart that you are one with God.

The opening affirmation at this service was: *I am here by divine appointment and God makes straight my way.*

The minister presented it as if it were a prime text straight out of the gospel according to Unity, which it was. We repeated it. We dwelt upon it in silence, and by that time the mood was one of sincere and deep reflection, and empathy was firmly established.

What makes an affirmation so powerful and instantaneous? Is it merely the positive, unquestioning manner in which it is spoken? Why are we caught so quickly in a sense of the Presence? I could say that in this case it was the Unity headquarters environment, the presence of Lowell seated next to me, and the pre-service that created my response.

It was something more—a matter of *consciousness.* An awareness pervaded the group that this is what should happen, does happen, when the presence of God is believed in to a point of cosmic attunement.

I cannot help contrasting this experience with the customary practice in the traditional churches and in my own pastorate experience. We of the "historic" faith open our worship with a processional, a choir rendition, a congregational hymn, or an invocation, "The Lord is in His Holy Temple, let all the earth keep silence before Him." We sing the Gloria and pray the Lord's Prayer, but somehow we fail to reach the person in the pew with the thrilling reminder that at this moment we are one with God in a very special close encounter.

In Protestantism, worship is based on the hope that the individual will participate. We liturgical Christians hold to this hope during the responsive readings, the Scripture readings, and the confession of faith. We seek to deepen the worship experience by way of the sermon. One would imagine that these would serve the purpose. But they do not. All too often the service remains stereotyped and impersonal. Many of my minister friends in these early 1960s complained that their people were apathetic and listless and that sixty percent of the members stayed away from the services because they didn't seem to "get anything out of it."

Perhaps the meaning has gone out of ritualistic symbolism. Perhaps time has sapped away the vitality and left tradition standing as a matter of form. Perhaps the ministry has lost its spiritual adventurousness. I have heard ministers complain about the agony of *preparing* a sermon! Could it be that Protestantism is no longer sufficiently prophetic or fired by spiritual ideas and that solemnized religions continue to perpetuate doctrines that lack contemporary relevance? In the historic churches the form is sacramental and the object of worship is God; in Unity the form is non-sacramental and the object of worship is one's oneness with God. There is never liturgy for the sake of liturgy in Unity or form for the sake of tradition. Worship is a state of consciousness with a cosmic touch.

My thoughts flashed back to the first Unity service I ever attended. It was a small group, meeting one Sunday morning in a cramped room in Chicago's Kimball Hall. I do not recall anything special about the woman minister or the order of service, but I remember that early in the service I found myself standing with the congregation, reciting aloud an affirmation so audacious that I could never get it off my mind: *The love of God manifests through me, and I am filled with light, wisdom, and peace.*

Never in all my churchgoing had I been told publicly that the love of God manifests through me, and never by any stretch of the imagination did I think I would ever declare it openly, aloud, and honestly. Nor did I ever tell my parishioners that this might be true for them. We occasionally felt these awarenesses, I am sure, in our aloneness; but we certainly never pooled them in a stream of consciousness and went public with them! I had stood for prayer in my parental church uncounted times with an urge to admit this *feeling* about the love of God manifesting, but it would have seemed like heresy to have confessed it aloud. And, furthermore, it used to be that whenever I felt filled with light, wisdom, and peace I always felt a certain pinch of egoism. God was not this kind of God, and worship was not this kind of worship. When many a good orthodox Christian is filled with "light, wisdom, and peace," there is often a feeling of fear, apprehension, and a remembrance of sins on the other side of the coin, as if God didn't really want us to be that happy and free.

In short, Unity affirmations used to seem too modern to me, too lacking in good evangelical humility! I could accept them from my standpoint of research but not from a personal "conversion" point of view. But a stream of Unity services had gone under the bridge of my spiritual quest since then, and at this moment of worship in Unity Village Chapel I realized that my response was changing, that it had changed through the years. A needed subjectivism was beginning to overrule objective investigation. This Unity headquarters service represented another step in that direction. *I am here by divine appointment!* kept running through my mind. Affirmations now dared me to see the best in me and, seeing it, to try to be my best. They challenged me to come closer to the light and to edge nearer to the heart of God.

Surely we have a right to expect something transcendent when we go to church. We have the right to be extolled as children of God. That is what the church is for. That is the true meaning of "church," a special community of special people, and not in any superior sense but in a knowledge of the discovery of one's true identity. That I missed this in my ministry was *my* problem. Here, in Unity, absorbed in the awareness of our "true being," we at least partially ascend to the top of the holy mount. When we close our eyes and say: *I am here by divine appointment and God makes straight my way,* we arouse these qualities within ourselves, in others, and in the world in which we live.

We hear and know enough about these negativisms throughout the workaday week. We carry on a daily struggle with our limitations, and there are sufficient reminders all around us that, instead of light, we are often in the dark, instead of wisdom, we are kept in ignorance, and in place of peace, we are presented with no alternative but war. So we come to church seeking the other side of things—and in Unity it is promised that those who come seeking shall find it in the metaphysical coin of the realm.

It is this quality of the quest that distinguishes metaphysical audiences from most other congregations and makes them easier to talk to, more attentive and eager for an interchange of ideas. Unity is, after all, a *school* of Christianity. Unity followers come to a service as students, to learn, to give, to share. They bring prayers in their hearts for the speaker. They are looking for things to live by and guideposts along the way. Among Unity members, few come to the services because they feel it is their duty. There is as yet no traditionalism in Unity which must be perpetuated, no fear of hell or divine retribution which must be appeased, no Sunday spiritual duties which must be kept because it is the thing to do. True Unity people come seeking, endeavoring to see the good and to improve their lives through their recognition of the Christ within.

Their belief or creed, if they have one, is concise and simple:

There is but one Mind in the universe, mortal mind is false or intellect. It gathers its information from without.

Universal Mind sees and speaks from within.

Our ways of thinking make our happiness or unhappiness, our success or nonsuccess.

We can, by effort, change our ways of thinking.

God is at all times, regardless of our so-called sins, trying to pour more good into our lives and to make them ever larger and more successful.

One method for pouring "more good into our lives" is by means of the Word, and by this is meant the positive, spoken word of faith. The term *Logos* in the sense that it means the Word of God made flesh in Jesus Christ may not be any clearer to Unity teachers than it is to traditional theologians, but Unity believes with all its heart that the actively expressed Logos as the *will of God* is identifiable with the individual.

Worship in Unity means entering into the spirit of the Word made flesh. Hence, the affirmations are not merely words, they are convictions about God articulated and breathed into life. They are cosmic forces spun on the vehicle of speech. The mind transmits them. Prayer may send them from one individual to another, but in worship they are communicated and expressed in one's true self and then absorbed and generated into action in the silence.

The minister at this service again employed the affirmation technique in his meditation when he said: *I am free. I am free from all thought of worry and anxiety, for I place myself and my affairs into God's keeping.*

After a brief exposition on these words, we were asked to repeat them thoughtfully with him, aloud, then softly, then mentally: *I am free from all thought of worry and anxiety, for I place myself and my affairs into God's keeping. I am free from all envy and resentment because God is my All in All. I am free...*

There are those who will say that the mere affirming of freedom does not open prison doors, that the chains are still there, and the problems have not been overcome. But to those who believe, to those who fix their minds on faith, every sense of bondage or burden is lifted when one turns to God and proclaims: *I am free! I am free from all thought of worry and anxiety, for I place myself and my affairs into God's keeping.*

At least, that was my conviction.

There is, as Unity insists, and as Jesus Christ promised, release from anxiety and worry when you realize that God is always with you and that you are never alone, that there is nothing too great for Him, that there is no problem that cannot be solved with His help. *Cast your burden upon the Lord...* (Psalms 55:22) *"the truth will make you free..."* (John 8:32) *"Whatever you ask in my name, I will do it..."* (John 14:13) These and innumerable similar texts Unity accepts literally because it understands them metaphysically.

This is worship—the act of paying divine honor to a Deity by taking Him at His word. This is worship—to honor with extravagant love the Deity's promises. This is worship—to recognize with unflinching courage the Truth that, since we have been made in the image and likeness of God, we share His nature.

Unity shares it through the Christ. Worship in this sense is essentially an art, and the techniques involved unfold intuitively. The greater the quest, the greater the meaning. What happens in the Unity church service is but a transcript of what happens whenever one worships. Worship represents the "tied to" place, the still point of the Spirit.

Unity believes it can be an actual place like a room or a chapel or a grove, an office or a mountaintop, or simply a state of consciousness. It can be a vibration to which you attune yourself. What is sought is that the rate of vibration be in harmony with the deepest experience of the meditation itself. Therefore, work can be worship. So can play. Tithing is worship. Blessing the offering, holding the offering in meditative gratitude, and affirming God's gifts are acts of worship. The point of fixation, as far as Unity is concerned, is the Christ within.

This Christ within is God personified, not formed into an image or set upon a wall, nor a God longing for routine prayers or liturgies rehearsed and dramatized. The Christ within is God working and walking with us because He lived as Man among us.

The Christ within is the I that I would be. Unity would say He is the Son of God whose sonship we clearly feel and know when we truly worship. The Christ is the expression of the best in us, the best that we in our upward climb have been able to perceive and in whose perception we perceive ourselves.

The Christ within is the Spirit of God incarnate, not something to explore or to explain or even to examine, but a Spirit to experience by the indwelling light which is the life of everyone. The Christ is and was a Power and a Presence known and to be known, whose secret source is ever waiting in the secret place of worship.

Our Unity service was an extension in depth of this estimate of worship and the Christ. The songs we sang were affirmative songs, positive in their appraisal of where we stand with God: "Perfect is my heart before Thee, Perfect walk I in Thy ways; Perfect love even now restores me, Perfect is my song of praise."

The sermon, which is the heart and core of the service, is not a sermon; it is a lesson; and when it ceases to be a lesson and becomes sermonic, it ceases to be Unity. It is an exposition of Truth as Unity sees Truth, a truth which is at the same time relative and absolute, that has no quarrel with other faiths, that is never in conflict with science, and that is consistently alert to new revelations.

The thesis for the lesson presented by the minister on this particular morning was based not on what was happening on the international, political, or economic fronts, but on what was taking place on the mental front in the minds of each of us. The concept was to trigger a recognition that in our individualized mental and spiritual worlds of mind, a breakthrough in consciousness is taking place. As this individualization is recognized, it leads to a breakthrough in the "collective unconscious" and effects changes in society and the world.

The lesson dealt with such striking things as the impartiality of God as opposed to God's favoritism. It spoke of the Christ power and the Christ word as being the essence of life. It pinned down the "Father and I are One" idea with force and conviction. There were warmth and logic and humor in the presentation, and I was happy to have been brought here by divine appointment.

I can sum up the impact of the lesson by saying that it presented the most positive side of the coin of the realm. There were no references to the highly inflated and much overstated "wages of sin."

The power of the Unity lesson is in direct ratio to the demonstration of Truth in the life of the speaker. The greatest Unity ministers are those who live the greatest lives of faith. This has nothing to do with eloquence, intellectual achievement, pulpit presence, or charisma. It is not even the word that does the work; it is the spirit within the word.

I know a woman whose effective ministry has built one of Unity's largest Florida churches. Hundreds come to hear her each week and thousands are influenced by the power of her faith. She has had many demonstrations of healing and was herself destined, according to medical diagnosis, to be a paralytic for life. She met this challenge on Jesus Christ's terms of healing and, like Charles Fillmore, bore no record of the past except a barely noticeable limp.

One day a newcomer to the city came to her for help. The minister counseled this woman in her church study and was able to help her with a health problem. When the conference was over and the minister rose to escort the woman to the door, the latter noticed that the minister limped slightly. Thoughtlessly the visitor remarked, "I came to you in the hope that you could effect a cure in me. Now I see that you have not even been able to heal yourself!"

The minister replied, "When Jesus died and rose again, He came with a new body, but it still bore the print of the nails. I, too, have risen from a disease for which I was told there was no hope. My limp is to me but the print of the nails."

This is the spirit behind Unity worship, an indomitable persistence working away at Unity truths.

I know a husband-wife team who have established a work so phenomenal that a Protestant church in the same city sent a delegation to discover the "techniques of their operation." The Protestant leaders could not understand how this young Unity couple with no seminary training, no oratorical or pulpit professionalism, and no traditional background could be so successful. The delegation never learned the reason. It was too simple and too uncatchable. The secret was in their spiritual consciousness with a cosmic touch, or shall we say cosmic consciousness? Their success lay in a provocative truth: *We receive in proportion to our use of that which we have.*

One Unity minister who fascinated me and who had an extraordinary following used none of the old techniques that ministers in the historic churches commonly subscribed to. He made no parish calls; he had no use for membership drives. He shunned financial campaigns and carried on no special social relationship with the members of his congregation. In fact, there were any number of people on his church roll who scarcely knew him. To analyze his success was impossible for those who did not understand Unity. They knew nothing of his intuitive power or of the fact that he carried his church in his heart. They knew even less of his firm conviction that when the Spirit of truth has come, *it* does the work. Even the minister himself may never have known what a clear channel he was for the transmission of the Spirit of God into the lives of those he blessed.

Success in Unity cannot be measured in terms of numbers or in the size of the congregation. The kingdom, as the Scripture states, comes not by observation. Unity has great churches with many members, and churches just as great with few members. Often a church is not even the reflection of the minister, it is the lengthened stature of the Unity idea, the belief that every individual is a child of God and that with proper nurture his divine potential can be realized and expressed. This is the power of Unity, and this is how Unity worships. Its worship is the surface manifestation of a subsurface consciousness.

I have been at Unity services and heard the people repeat the affirmation: *Unity is growing, growing, growing!* As they affirmed this, one could feel the growth. You could see the churches rising from small groups of believers to great congregations of doers. Such churches bore the Unity name: Unity at the Crossroads of the World (New York City); Unity-by-the-Sea; Unity of the Palm Beaches; Unity Christ Church; Unity Church of Christ; Christ Church Unity; Unity Center of Truth; Unity Truth Center; Unity Church of the Valley; Unity Church of the Oaks; Lakeside Unity; Unity of Miami, of Chicago, of Cleveland, of Oklahoma City, of Detroit, of Dallas, of Escondido, of Des Moines, of Milwaukee, of New Orleans, of Spokane, of Boston, of your hometown and mine.

And all the people said: *Unity is growing,*

growing, growing! and Unity grew.

The young minister was on good target from the opening conviction of divine appointment to the premise that, as the individual is changed, the world begins to change, and, as the simple rudiments of Jesus Christ's teachings are understood and demonstrated, the new age is ushered in.

The world is "saved" as individuals are "saved." If one person could do it alone, then the beginning of the Christian era or the years of the life of Jesus would surely have resulted in His hope of peace on Earth, good will to men. But the world en masse—politically, internationally, militarily—was not much different after He left than when He came. Individuals had been touched and changed spiritually, and ideologically, but not sufficiently in depth and not enough in number to effect the miracle that will bring to pass the new heaven and the new Earth of the Messianic dream.

The challenge, therefore, remains personal; and Unity, despite its drift toward churchification, remains the advocate of a personalized faith.

And so the service ended with a personalized blessing, Unity's immortal Prayer of Protection. Unity people everywhere know this prayer and love it and use it. Ever since it was channeled through the mind of Unity's James Dillet Freeman, it has been an unbroken thread, as far as my remembrance is concerned, from my first visit to Unity headquarters on Tracy Avenue until this present moment.

More popular now than ever, the prayer has been heard wherever Unity is known in the world and, literally, as history has recorded, even beyond the reach of planet Earth. The prayer was carried, in July 1969, to the surface of the moon by pilot Edwin A. Aldrin, Jr., when he stepped from Apollo II in its historic lunar flight.

We are standing now, hands joined, throughout Unity Village Chapel, united in Unity, affirming together:

The Light of God surrounds me,
The Love of God enfolds me,
The Power of God protects me,
The Presence of God watches over me.
Wherever I am, God is!

Chapter III

The Unity Approach to Prosperity

One morning at Unity Village when I awoke to the sound of rain on the motel roof, I caught myself saying, "God's rain," and got to thinking how in the Unity environment a person is inclined to spiritualize and psychoanalyze events as to the part they play in the game of life. And there was no denying the lift that this kind of approach gave to the game.

God's rain, for example.

Or other things, like prayers, shall we say.

Like a prayer I heard children praying in a Unity Sunday school: "Our happy hearts just sing and sing! We thank You, God, for everything!" It became one of my favorite blessings. Another prayer I learned from Unity children is superb for mealtime: "We thank Thee, Lord, for happy hearts, for fair and sunny weather. We thank Thee, Lord, for this our food, and that we are together!" I remember using it in a group when it was snowing outside and marveled how automatically I changed the words to, "We thank Thee, Lord, for this lovely *snowy* weather."

Or today, for this lovely rainy weather.

That is the Unity idea.

We thank Thee, Lord, for everything—snow, rain, fair weather, any weather. Unity has a subtle way of returning us worldlings to an age of religious innocence.

These are excellent thoughts with which to begin the day—any day.

The big, impersonal world loses some of its bite in metaphysical thinking. The issues of life become less culpable, and our goals are given a highly God-centered perspective. Even prosperity, which to many people has been considered out of bounds in their God relationship, has now become a subject for seminars and workshops, not only in metaphysical fields but throughout the length and breadth of the religious world.

In Unity you are assured that money can be the root of good instead of evil. You need never think of profitable business deals as being outside of God's sphere or of success as being beyond your capabilities.

Taking a brief rather than a lingering backward look, the better to understand the present, I recognized that Unity looked upon God's gift of money as it did upon God's gift of rain. *It was abundantly free,* especially to those who understood the working of the law and who had the proper will to "accept their good," and most particularly to those who had the spirit to bless money and use it as an extension of God's gift.

Charles Fillmore was emphatically articulate about prosperity and extended the term to embrace not only money but life in all its phases and forms. *Charge your mind,* he said, *with statements that express plenty. Deny poverty. Praise what you have, be it ever so little, and insist that it is constantly growing larger.*

I read into this that we must be grateful for what we have before we can expect to be trusted with more. And I appreciated the whimsical parable Papa Charley once culled from a happening in the Deep South.

"There was a pastor in a small church in Georgia," he reported, "who suggested to his congregation of cotton farmers that they dedicate a tenth part of their land to the Lord and ask Him for protection against the ravages of the boll weevil which had devastated the crops in that vicinity for several years. Seven farmers decided to do this. They set aside a tenth part as the Lord's land and though they took no measures to protect their crop on these dedicated acres, the boll weevil did not attack the cotton there. Futhermore, the quality of the fiber was better on those acres than on any that adjoined them. The experiment was so successful that practically all the farmers in that community decided to follow the plan in the future."

I liked that story. I liked to feel that God was pleased with the telling. I liked it for its closeness to nature and for the hint that there are telltale signs of heaven's presence to be found in many places.

God's rain, for example.

And God's land.

And no more boll weevils.

The parable aptly defined Unity's position in relation to both money and "miracles." The regenerated fields were not a supernatural phenomenon. They represented logical consequences of an immutable law. God protects what is His and blesses what is blessed to Him.

Money is a touchstone in the working of this law. It is often *the* touchstone, for there are people all over the world who are Christians only up to their hip pockets. They give the Lord practically everything in the way of advice, excuses, good intentions, even time, and a certain amount of energy, everything excepting the "almighty dollar." They shy away from stewardship, which is why they are annoyed by boll weevils.

Unity was telling us that we are dealing not with a supranormal, anthropomorphic God but with a law, a law which says that money has a spiritual as well as a material side, and that the spiritual is the "cause side." The spiritual side has to do with stewardship whether you are a cotton farmer or a financier. The "cause side" creates the conditions in which you live in your environmental world.

To dwell upon poverty is to create it.

To dwell upon abundance is to attract it.

Spiritual economics, according to metaphysical teachings, suggest that our attitude about life fashions the "money world" in which we live.

If you give grudgingly, you surround yourself with grudging thoughts.

If you give poorly, you remain poor.

You evolve according to the preform of your thoughts.

Consciousness makes you what you are, and it is up to you to make your consciousness, or, rather, to recognize your consciousness as God's manifestation.

It occurred to me that Unity people are

never poor, neither in spirit nor in worldly goods. Etched on their hearts is a major tenet in their canon of beliefs: "Wealth of consciousness will express itself in wealth of manifestation." Here in the environment of Unity Village this seemed to me an infallible decree falling, like God's rain, on the unjust and the just, nourishing and refreshing the subsoil of faith in the human heart. "Wealth of consciousness will express itself in wealth of manifestation."

Long ago in my insistence that I could fit Unity teachings into my traditional evangelical indoctrination, I learned a prosperity prescription consisting of four simple steps:

1. Recognize that there is no lack and that the law of cause and effect operates interdependently in all of life.

2. Affirm thoughts of abundance in the assurance that these thoughts are irrevocably true and workable for you.

3. Translate the thoughts into action.

4. Give thanks for the demonstration of Truth.

Recognize. Affirm. Translate. Give Thanks. Who could doubt its practical use? Only those who would not try it. Who would call it simple and naive? Only those who missed its implications. Who could limit its power? Only those who put a limit on God. *Recognize. Affirm. Translate. Give Thanks.*

I worked with that formula and found that it worked! Which is usually the way with the metaphysical injunctions I have tried.

Unity lives by this prescription religiously and demonstrates it convincingly. It is one of the affirmational procedures by which the growth of the movement is charted. It is one of the reasons that the Unity I was visiting now was a Village fully incorporated, proving the soundness of the formula and the working of the law. To understand all this it is necessary to recognize one incontrovertible Truth: *God's substance is unlimited,* and begin to live that way.

Substance in the Unity sense is not to be confused with materiality. Substance is not some *thing* or entity or specific material. Substance is the "God stuff," the divine distillate, out of which all reality is formed, the intangible essence back of all matter and force.

Metaphysics never idealized poverty as did the early Christian saints or the Hindu sannyasin or the Buddhist monks. Metaphysicians never sang the song on which I was nurtured during the formative years of my youth:

A tent or a cottage
What do I care?
They're building a place
For me over there.

None of the "over there," pie-in-the-sky fervor ever crept into the modern Unity movement, not even through the back door. Eternal substance, like eternal life, was here and now waiting to be materialized. Granted that some metaphysical leaders had patrons who funded their work and contributors without whom their churches might not have been built, but Unity's success was not founded on a monetary measurement, and you will be told that the patron's support was itself the working of the law.

Before coming to Unity on this occasion, I had discussed the subject of prosperity with Dr. Charles S. Braden, who was known and respected by religious leaders both in and out of the metaphysical field. Braden was a fellow researcher in contemporary religions, fully accredited, with books scholarly and thoroughly documented. Methodist ordained, missionary, minister, and university professor, he was of the opinion that Unity "avoided wherever possible any semblance of commercialization." Never was God looked upon as a servitor from whom one sought largesses, or an alchemist who made men rich because they chanted a magical creed. God as Spirit and Creator was Author of the law, the law which affirmed that if you understand the nature of substance and follow the Christ principles, and give the Lord His tithe, the heavens open.

Prosperity is like falling rain.

Consecrate the acres, dedicate the land, and you get rid of the boll weevils.

I had to admit that through the years Unity's prosperity premises had literally enriched my life. They helped me get rid of a sense of lack and limitation on God's part. I grew up with the belief that God's good was measurable, like grain in a bin, and that there was just so much grain to go around. I had it fixed in my mind that each of us had been given a scoop of a certain size, and that mine was just big enough or small enough to help me "get by" in this highly competitive world. Then I took a long leap toward a new belief. *God's resources are unlimited.* I had *not* arbitrarily been given a scoop of a certain size. My capacity for prosperity in its various forms—talent, money, productivity—was unlimited. God's substance did not fluctuate with the times. It did not decrease during depressions and rise when the market was up.

God's resources were ever the same—constant, abundant, freely circulating, available to all.

Furthermore, I realized as I never had before that, "Money is the materialization of ideas." This principle shifted my sporadic views about prosperity into a semblance, at least, of stabilized thinking.

For me, tithing was the big breakthrough. And that, when I think about it, was a funny thing. I had been taught and urged in the seminary to get "my people" to tithe when I got into the ministry. The need for tithing had been made clear: Tithing was the life-blood of religion, for without contributions how could you get missionaries into the field to spread the gospel; how could you build churches and educational units; how could you get your people to pay your salary if they didn't tithe? I have admitted, since my experience in the Wabash Avenue church, that I preached tithing so hard I almost started to tithe myself. But I didn't, because I did not understand the meaning of tithing, that it is a stewardship and a partnership with God apart from sending out missionaries or building churches or spreading the denominational gospel. It is a covenant and a commitment to the Giver of all good who for some reason loves a cheerful tither.

Unity's pocket-sized cardboard prosperity bank was, for me, an early step in the experiment. Lowell gave me several of these neat, beautifully decorated, foldaway banks during one of our meetings. Lowell actually "invented" this ever-popular tithing box, and Rick did the first art work on it.

One time, on a trip to my parental home in Sauk City, Wisconsin, I took the prosperity bank with me. There I discovered that our local church had just introduced the envelope system as its money-raising method. My mother, the only woman member on the church consistory, was actively engaged in this latest approach to church finances, and she explained that now our members needed only to tuck their weekly contributions into the handy multi-colored envelope and drop it into the collection plate each Sunday morning. She thought it would inspire people to come to the services more regularly. It did. But it also caused some to stay away.

My mother was head of the every-member-canvass which put the envelope system into operation, and one Sabbath afternoon her crews fanned out over town, dedicated to the task of persuading church members to pledge a weekly contribution. When I signed my pledge for my home church, I shared with my mother the plan of Unity's prosperity bank and how the daily tithe helps a person to get subscriptions to Unity periodicals and makes you feel you are part of its prayer service and so on.

My mother interrupted by saying: "But you don't belong to Unity, I hope!"

I put her mind at rest.

"How much do you put into it?" she asked, with some concern.

"A quarter a day."

For a moment she was relieved—until she did some figuring. "That," she said, "would be over ninety dollars a year. That is more than some of our richest members give to our church. Why is it that our people don't give the way they should?"

"It's a matter of consciousness," I said.

"Consciousness?" she echoed. "Our people are just too stingy, that's all!"

She examined the prosperity bank. It was a new departure for her to think that giving involved a law, and she also felt there was a bit of audacity involved in the declarations: *Divine love bountifully supplies and increases this my offering!* and *I am always provided for because I have faith in God as my omnipresent abundance!* Only someone as orthodox as my mother knew how revolutionary all this sounded to orthodox ears.

One feature about the bank impressed her—the ritual. Unity might not have called it a ritual, but my mother did. A ritual. She liked the idea of holding a quarter in her hand, placing the coin partway into the slot, closing her eyes, and whispering a prayer. She loved to pray, especially in German, a language which she was sure was considerably dearer to the Lord than English.

She thought Unity was wise in combining the giving of the gift with the praying of a prayer. With all her solid religiosity, she had never thought about blessing the contributions she made to the Lord's work. She had her policies, such as never using a gloved hand to drop an offering into the collection plate, never putting in loose change, and certainly never glancing to see what the person seated next to her contributed, unless perhaps it might have been my father. She often quietly checked up on him, but usually she simply closed her eyes and let the offering fall. It had always been a duty. Now it became a ritual.

Persuading her to get the feel of the prosperity bank, I asked her to repeat the affirmation: *God is in charge of all my affairs, and*

abundant good is manifested daily for me.
She was a good sport, for I suspect this was
the most positive affirmation my mother had
ever said aloud. Fifty years of German evangelical indoctrination had persuaded her that
God might *not* be in charge of all her affairs.
After all, the devil might have a hand in
them. And as for abundant good being manifested daily, she was not so sure about that
either. She often felt beset by abundant evil.
Furthermore, an affirmation of this kind was
like putting words into God's mouth, or at
least telling Him what He ought to do, and
our family had been rigorously brought up on
"... *not my will, but thine.* ... " (Luke 22:42)
But she went through with it. She spoke the
words and dropped the coin, and it seemed to
me she did it with a sense of real exhilaration.

We often talked about it later as the years
of my research developed and as I frequently
returned home with reports of what was happening among the new religions which, like
Unity, had staked their claims in the religious
culture of our time.

"There *is* something wrong with us," she
would murmur, referring to "us" as traditional Protestants in general. "There is surely
something wrong with our benevolences.
Even the envelope system hasn't solved the

problem. Our people just simply aren't good givers."

Rummage sales, baked goods sales, soup suppers, pancake breakfasts, even church bazaars never got the budget over the hump. There was also the period when fast-talking salesmen used the church parlors to demonstrate stainless steel pots and pans, giving the church a seemingly generous cut; but this, too, never seemed to get the blessing of the Lord, nor the blessing of my mother. She was dead set against turning the church into a "sales barn" as she called it. (Wasn't this why Jesus drove the moneychangers out of the temple?)

Meantime, Unity was growing. Unity was prospering. *Recognize. Affirm. Translate. Give Thanks.*

This matter of prosperity in terms of dollars and cents was much maligned by the established churches, particularly during the 1960s and '70s. Traditional church leaders generally, and fundamentalists in particular, accused Unity and other truth movements of commercialism and religious merchandising because of their emphasis on "material prosperity" while overlooking the poverty and suffering among the world's underprivileged and not sending out missionaries to save the unsaved in "foreign lands." Preaching and promoting prosperity was, they said, self-righteous arrogance and humanistic materialism.

The sudden publication boom following Norman Vincent Peale's book in the 1950s caused fundamentalists, and many establishment clergy as well, to accuse this Reformed Church minister of selling out to New Thought thinking. Unity principles, it was said, were being promoted by this Marble Collegiate Church minister, as though they belonged in religious programming, when actually they were nothing more than what Peale had titled them, "The Power of Positive Thinking," and a secularization of religious principles.

But Dr. Peale was not the only utilizer-advocate of metaphysical techniques. There were, as earlier mentioned, Methodists such as Dr. Dunnington, Episcopalians such as the Reverend Robert A. Russell, Presbyterians such as Glenn Clark, religious innovators such as Claude M. Bristol and Frank B. Robinson, plus Unitarians and several Catholic priests who eventually became Unity ministers. All of this caused the emphasis on prosperity to roll through many traditional churches like a gilt-edged stock straight from the brokerage of God and man.

And here was I having authored a book on Unity in 1962 in which I confessed I wondered just how the good Lord *did* regard prosperity when it came to dollars and cents. Prosperity affirmations, as before mentioned, had definitely not been part of my ministerial training. I was by no means ready to say unequivocally that, "Jesus Christ is now here, raising me to His consciousness of the omnipresent, all-proving God substance, and my prosperity is assured!"

I realized how wide my early training had made the gap between God and mammon. And what was that about the rich man having as much difficulty getting into heaven as a camel had in getting through the eye of a needle, or however the biblical reference phrased it?

Some ministers in the established churches were convinced that God had never condemned money, and they had *their* rationale and their Scripture texts to prove it. Others said He sanctified money and they had *their* texts and *their* rationale. But no matter what views about money ministers held deep in their heart of hearts, they wanted to see their churches and their ministries prosper, and financial increase was usually a tacit endorsement of the Lord's good favor. All of which accounted for the fact that many a minister turned inquisitively to Unity to discover what made it prosper and grow. Some misread the signals, a few caught on to the secret, but some delved deeply and sincerely into the adventure that said: *Recognize. Affirm. Translate. Give Thanks. And tithe!*

One thing was clear. In the wake of a popularization of metaphysical teachings about prosperity, the churches of America, regardless of their denominational identities, were facing a moment of truth: Either spiritualize money or make some other kind of reconciliation between the animosity of God and mammon, because the gap no longer existed in the public mind. Either admit that God, as the source of supply, does not construe money as a tool of Satan, or admit that you are using psychological techniques as suggested by secular entrepreneurs. For America was being bombarded not only by positive thinking, but by goal-setting advocates announcing courses through the magic of believing that "Mind Makes Millionaires" and "You Can Be One, Too." A rash of prosperity principles from the flourishing mills of Napoleon Hill, Dale Carnegie, Orison

Marden, Earl Nightingale, and many more spanned the years, accomplishing their own goal-setting objectives. And where did the spiritualization of these prosperity ideas originate? Almost without exception from the metaphysical field.

The implication in all this was neither simple nor conclusive until one reread the Unity texts and stayed with the Unity principles. In so doing, one was compelled to look upon money as a symbol of God's supply and use money as the objectification of spiritual substance to be employed not for personal aggrandizement or denominational superiority but for the expression of God's kingdom, and to advance the teachings of the Christ. *And tithe!*

Whatever American Christendom was to become in the last quarter of the 20th century, it was clear that churches-at-large became prosperity minded and needed to make no apologies to a society which had long since adapted an ideology to which the clergy, for good or ill, was just now coming into awareness. It would not be long before even the most fundamentalistic groups would be using metaphysical prosperity principles. This often meant patterning them to their own interpretations while still condemning and misquoting Unity and other movements in the New Thought field. Yet this—the field of metaphysics—was the laboratory from which a new era in Christian ethics was launched and demonstrated. It also gave rise to the growing question of whether society influences religion or religion society. And Unity's founders said: *The possessions of the Father are not in stocks and bonds but in the divine possibilities implanted in the mind and soul of every person. Through the mind ideas are brought into being. Through the soul God's wealth of love finds its expression. The mind is the crucible in which the ideal is transcended into the real.*

And when they said this, what did *they* have in mind, an American millionaire, or a millionaire like Jesus?

Definitely, the latter.

This is how early Unity impressed itself on me and my idealism. Prosperity was not a matter of money. It was, as has been said, a matter of the spirit of man recognizing itself as the Spirit of God working His will with "substance," according to the light of Truth.

Questions that had annoyed me in my pastorate, such as how to raise money without being accused of commercialism, how to advance the work of the church without falling victim to the taint of promotionalism, how to deal with money, and how far money should be permitted to deal with me, Unity answered with a single phrase, "Religion is God's business in the world and you are His partner in this business."

With this realization, as far as I was concerned, ideas became synonymous with the coin of the realm. To rightly assess one's prosperity, it was necessary to take an inventory of the ideas stored in consciousness. The total wealth of life was therefore already ours, needing only the manifestation of the ideal into the real.

The power of affirmations lay in the fact that they trained the subconscious to react to the realization of the goal affirmed. When I proclaimed: *I have faith in the substance of God working in and through me to increase and bring abundance into my world,* my faith started to work in the mind substance and make me prosperous. Prosperity meant work, but not in the frantic, frenzied whir of life. It meant work first of all in the tranquil world of ideas which is ever ready and waiting to help us receive what we rightly claim as our own.

This "right to claim" was one of the most helpful of all hints in my upward climb toward a new belief. It carried me over many a deep-seated preoccupation which had long been a part of my nature. For example, I had always been tempted to depend upon others for my security. I always hoped that some-day someone would come along and subsidize me or underwrite or finance me, though the reason was never quite clear. I didn't actually subscribe to the concept that the world owes me a living, but I certainly dreamed about it.

Unity helped diagnose my condition in bold golden print when it said: *The other fellow's realization of substance will not guarantee your supply. You must become conscious of it for yourself. Identify yourself with substance until you make it yours; it will change your finances, destroy your fears, stop your worries, and you will soon begin to rejoice in the ever-present bounty of God.*

The words were for me. They were a finger singling me out. The statement was something more. It was an epitaph over a self that I was bound and determined to make short shrift of once and for all. And I did. I recognized *substance.* I *recognized* that there is no lack, and I recognized that the law of cause and effect operates interdependently in all of life. I *affirmed* thoughts of abundance in the assurance that these thoughts are true and workable for me. I *translated* the thoughts into action. I *gave thanks* for the demonstration of Truth. And the moment I followed this formula, everyone, it seemed, wanted to do something for me!

It was a great leap, and one that I was eager to recommend to others. I wanted to say, as Charles Fillmore had said, "Be still and turn within to the great Source. See with the eye of faith that the whole world is filled with substance. See it falling all about you as snowflakes of gold and silver and affirm with assurance: *I have unbounded faith in the all-present spiritual substance increasing and multiplying at my word.*"

Recognize. Affirm. Translate. Give Thanks.

The symbolic promise of the windows of heaven being opened for those who bring their tithes into the storehouse means that the mind (heaven) is filled to overflowing with creative and productive ideas. Tithing, according to Unity, means more than merely putting a tenth of one's earning to work for the Lord; it means recognizing that all of one's money, possessions, talent, love, and time are God's substance over which we are stewards for a while. Such are the ingredients in the prosperity ideal. Such are the goals toward which the consecrated life must strive before being bold enough to affirm: *I claim the will of God for me to be rich, prosperous, and successful!*

I had always liked the phrase, "falling about you as snowflakes of gold and silver." But on this Thursday I was more inclined to say, "falling about you like rain."

God's rain . . . "

Chapter IV

How Unity Heals the Sick

Among the mail forwarded to me during my stay at Unity Village was a letter which said: *Our son Stephen has shown remarkable improvement in the last two months. Our prayers and the prayers of those who have prayed with us have been answered. It is only now that we begin to realize how much a strong faith in the power of God has meant and means to us. This was particularly significant for us all through the Lenten season. Silent Unity gave us an inspiring prayer:* You are God's whole and perfect child. Every cell in your body is aglow with His light, life, and love. *Thank you for helping us along a very difficult road.*

Stephen's case had been diagnosed by physicians as leukemia. I had heard the story from the boy's father, an engineering professor in a Western university. There had been the customary clinical consultations, the shock of the diagnosis, the need for conveying the report to Stephen's mother, the grief and frustration, then the anxiety and gloom which struck the household.

The parents' question was the inevitable, "Why?" Why should an eleven-year-old, a quiet, religiously minded boy, be stricken with this seemingly incurable disease? The attitude of the parents was typical of those who from childhood have been urged and warned to trust in God. Now in their attempt to understand this tragedy, they saw God through a glass even darker than Scripture had foretold.

What kind of a God is God? A God who meted out justice? Then what had Stephen done to warrant this "justice"? A God of mercy? Then why this inexorable medical pronouncement? "Your boy has eight months to a year to live," they had been told. Why? This was the cry with which the father and mother stormed the implacable wall which countless others, under similar circumstances, have frantically assailed.

I had occasion to tell the father about Unity, particularly Silent Unity, saying I was convinced that their records and research bore out the fact that spiritual healing is a reality. I was as sure of this as I was sure of "miracles" generally, for in my years of delving into the mystery of this field, all the way from the grotto at Lourdes to the tent meetings of faith healers, I had found too many testimonies and too much evidence to write off these cures as fiction, as medical remissions, or as psychosomatic, or as illusion.

I tried to explain to Stephen's father that healing phenomena, though they might be beyond the ordinary course of events, were never beyond the laws of nature or divine law, and that the miraculous must be adjudged in ratio to the degree in which these laws are understood. It is not tautological to say that miracles are for those who believe in them, for this is actually part of the process.

Spiritual healing, I contended, is for those who have the necessary will to believe. It is for those wise men of God, often called fools in the eyes of the world, who with steady, solid steps walk *free from fear,* and this may be the greatest miracle of all.

Which brings us to Unity.

Unity says: *I am made in the image and likeness of God. My body expresses His perfection in every detail.*

Repeat this, believing. Repeat this, accepting it as Truth. Repeat this in the confidence that nothing can deter you, and you will find that you are first of all casting out fear. Sickness, evil, and the devil in his many forms are not entities in Unity as they are in many religions; they are errors in the understanding of Truth. They are fear factors and must be denied.

Denials are a unique part of Unity's healing process. They are prologues to the use of affirmations, as if you were gently sweeping away cobwebs from the mind. Designed to get rid of the dust of doubt and fear, denials in Unity are a method of driving out pernicious illusions which may be blocking the path of healing.

I deny the belief that I have inherited disease, sickness, ignorance, or any mental limitation! is a popular Unity denial, and it is to be stated with the power and conviction of an affirmation.

I deny the belief that I am a child of the flesh and that I must suffer the sins of my forefathers unto the third and fourth generations. This is a denial open to criticism by the traditional church but strongly defended by Unity. Any other interpretation would be contrary to the law of Truth.

I deny that I have inherited the consequences of fear from my ancestors, or that the race can reflect its fears upon me.

This denial reminded me that I had to deny the fact that I inherited migraine headaches from my mother, a belief that had haunted me for many years. Especially since I was born on her birthday! It was commonplace for me to be told, "You come by your headaches naturally. Your mother has them, and you are bound to have them, too."

"Deny!" says Unity, and this became part of my learning and my "cure."

"Deny the morbid, the negative, the *untrue*. Clear away the cobwebs. Get rid of the dust. Make straight the way so that the great Physician can do His work, for it is He who does the healing. Invoke His presence with the Lord's Prayer. Talk to Him as though He were present. The first move in all healing," Unity suggests, "is the recognition on the part of the healer and on the part of the patient that God is present as all-powerful Mind."

In Unity, spiritual healing is not merely a real cure for imaginary diseases or an imaginary cure for real diseases; it is the fulfillment of the working of a law by those conversant with and obedient to the law.

Actually, it is more than a law. It is a divine principle at the heart of which is the reference just made: *freedom from fear*. Healing is in direct proportion to the degree in which healer and patient can remove fear from the patient and healer. Both Unity's denials and affirmations are directed toward effecting this consciousness. Drive out the deep-seated, subconscious fear by affirming: *My trust is in God, I am not afraid. His all-wise, all-loving, all-adjusting power fills me with enduring health and strength.* Banish anxiety with this unshaken conviction that: *God wants me to be well so that I can more perfectly do His will.*

Unity rids people of the lurking sense of guilt or misplaced contention that healing is not for them, urging them to affirm: *Health is my normal condition. Health is a condition true to the reality of my being.* This is one of Unity's strongest healing affirmations, for it assures patients that *nature* is always on their side. *Good* is always on their side. *God* is always on their side.

A woman afflicted with an eye injury was greatly helped by the assurance that the eye *wills to be well.* She had always believed that every cell and fiber of the body wills to be well, but the eye, she thought, was something different. The eye, she supposed, was given to deterioration instead of healing, and when this assumption was denied and she affirmed the Truth that the nature of the eye *is* health, she found an aid in dispelling the fear that the eye would not heal. She affirmed: *The light of life is the eye, and God is that light.*

There are Unity members who diligently perform eye exercises, believing that the eyes can be strengthened through proper care and diet and by means of specific techniques such as palming, blinking, gently sunbathing the eyes, and other practices which can be found in books in this specific field. All spiritual healers are slightly frustrated when they make claims for all sorts of cures and then find that they are helpless when it comes to presbyopia! Many have been the times that I have listened to practitioners of one type or other tell about marvelous healings and the limitlessness of faith, only to be asked by someone in the audience, "Then why do you wear glasses?"

Unity members also wear glasses, but within Unity's ranks are individuals who improve their eyesight with determined discipline and who effectively put off wearing glasses with the affirmation: *I deny all belief in failing eyesight. My eyes are the eyes of Spirit, strong, youthful, clear-sighted, and perfect.*

That is how Unity heals.

It heals by turning the table on disease.

In the face of a rash of ads warning us that we must expect at least two sick spells per year, and in defiance of the TV medicine men who fill the hearts and homes of Americans with the consciousness that the flu is out to get you and that colds are here to stay, Unity stands up to affirm: *I do not believe in weakness, inefficiency, or negativeness of any kind. I am a strong, bold, fearless, free spirit, and I am filled with the energy, vigor, and vitality of omnipresent, omnipotent Life.*

Given time, right thinking may even do away with the common cold.

But whether it does or not, Unity continues to broadcast its unswerving conviction that harmony is health, and health is harmony.

It sets the law of healing into action through the recognition: *My life is God's life.*

It draws unto itself the breath of life by insisting: *I freely, steadily breathe the vital essence of God's life, and by His life I am perfectly healed.*

No wonder, then, that Silent Unity said to Stephen's parents and to the boy: *You are God's whole and perfect child. Every cell in your body is aglow with His light, life, and love.*

In all of which Unity recognized the *fact* of sickness. *Truth* it might not have been, this leukemia, but *fact* it surely was. Unity recognizes the fact of sickness as it does the fact of

210

darkness, but it knows that if you approach darkness realistically with light, it will be shown that darkness is but an absence of light, as sickness is an absence of health. In this way Unity is a study of the true nature of things and believes that it is God's good will to "demonstrate over sickness."

The Bible has its own evidence for the working of this principle. Once a sightless man groped his way through Palestine streets, and those who watched him wondered why he was blind. They surmised that God was punishing him for some hidden sin or victimizing him because of the transgressions of his parents. When an itinerant Teacher came that way, someone called out to Him: *"Rabbi, who sinned, this man or his parents, that he was born blind?"* To which the Teacher said: *"It was not that this man sinned, nor his parents, but that the works of God might be made manifest in him..."* (John 9:2, 3) And the Teacher healed him.

This miracle of Jesus is descriptive of Unity's approach to healing. It cannot be said too often: You must get rid of the fear that God is a wrathful God. You must get rid of the anxiety that God is a merciless God. You must deny the mistaken and deeply ingrained apprehension that you are the victim of a capricious and wanton Creator who delights in afflicting the children of men. In the deepest moment of despair you must hear the words: *You are God's whole and perfect child. Every cell in your body is aglow with His light, life, and love.*

There is something besides fear that holds back healing. It is the age-old doctrine that we are destined to suffer along the way of life, that it has always been this way and will continue so to be. Here, again, Unity boldly denies the supposition. But it is ready to admit that suffering exists, and most Unity students will agree that the quest for healing may be a path for a new discovery of God.

The quest for healing inspires some to analyze their habits and their lives to see whether they are in harmony with God and His laws. Suffering may give us a new perspective on our sense of values. It may offer an insight into our deepest hidden responses, hidden so deeply that only the blunt key of sudden misfortune is able to open the door.

But having admitted and agreed to all this, Unity approaches sickness, suffering, and disease with the basic assurance that God will not willfully tempt His children with evil, nor annoy them with pain, nor terrorize them with tragedy. Unity teaches that, though suffering and sickness may be common to all humankind, they are not inevitable.

Most people, however, have been so saturated with the belief that suffering is part of God's will that they cannot visualize a world or an individual without it. This is the dust cloud hovering over many persons who seek spiritual healing. Unity may assure them that those who are masters of their faith are masters of their health, but all too often both religion and medicine will not let us forget that suffering is universal and that sickness is as much a part of every life as death.

The historic churches have been especially active in deifying suffering. They have continually called upon us to remember the Proverb: *My son, do not despise the Lord's discipline* (Prov. 3:11) and promoted the literal interpretation of the Psalmist who said: *I know, O Lord that thy judgments are right, and that in faithfulness thou hath afflicted me.* (Psalms 119:75) Young people have been catechized with the familiar text: . . . *for the Lord reproves him whom He loves.* (Prov. 3:12) These words always disturbed me because I wondered why, if the chastening was of the Lord and if it truly was an act of love, we should not calmly submit and ride it out, as it were. No one seemed to be doing this.

Even the most religious of my friends resisted divine chastening. At the slightest sign of sickness among the faithful, doctors were summoned, specialists were called, and all material means were rallied to fight against the Lord's decree.

When medical men were consulted, they corroborated what the clergy had proposed. Sickness, they agreed, was universal, and there was no escaping the fact that disease, like death, was part of the divine plan. Soon they supplied us with statistics. One out of every five, we were warned, could expect to be a cancer victim. One out of every six was ripe for a coronary. One out of every seven would be a casualty to muscular dystrophy. One member of every family could expect to spend one week annually in a hospital.

The statistics helped make it all come to pass, as statistics always do when enough people fix them firmly in mind. Hospitals to meet the statistics are feverishly built, and billboards to help frighten the public into meeting statistical prognostications can be seen all over. The drug industry becomes the largest and most aggressive cartel in the land. Individuals, inundated by pressure from preacher to pharmaceutical expert, feel they do not have a chance. They finally give up and give in, persuaded that they must learn to live with sickness and disease as we are learning to live with war and the apparent inability of international statesmen to effect a lasting peace.

Unity in no way rules out the reality of the world of the sick. The Fillmores had experienced this world. So have Unity ministers and Unity people. So have we all. We have all been faced with the challenge of it.

There is nothing in Unity that forbids a person going to a doctor. Unity believes that God works through medicine and through medical and non-medical professions dedicated to healing. The question as to where one should draw the line between medical aid and complete reliance on divine healing is not clearly resolved. Every minister, in fact every Unity affiliate, must make a personal decision as to how God's will and human skills work together. Some Unity teachers settle the problem by saying, "You cannot draw these fine lines. All is God and God is all."

Then comes the knotty question, "What about inoculations, blood transfusions, cold shots, miracle drugs, and all the rest?" Is such dependence a denial of one's faith in God? Is God in the penicillin, in the cortisone, in the tranquilizers? Unity says that you must decide. You must listen to your guidance. You must learn. You must live and act in accordance with your highest consciousness in the matter.

I have found that Unity agrees that unless we get at the true cause of our dilemmas through a spiritual analysis, we are making concessions to our weakness. Every time we take an aspirin without analyzing why we have the headache, we have slipped back a step in our conquest of self. Whenever we fail to heed the warnings about the dangers of certain drugs, their wrong use, their overuse, their needless use, we are attempting to circumvent Truth. And whenever we forfeit self-discipline, self-help, and obedience to nature's laws in favor of some quick and questionable chemical cure, we are trying to by-pass God's laws and self-responsibility.

Actor John Payne told me about his automobile accident in New York City. He had just stepped into the street when a careening car struck him with such force that he was tossed through the windshield and thrown to the curb. His scalp was badly cut, his face lacerated, bits of glass had lodged in his eyes, and one leg was shattered. As he lay there, he found himself overwhelmingly strengthened by what he referred to as "the truth of Unity teachings."

Affirmations passed through his mind, sustaining him. In a most remarkable way he *knew* that *life, strength, and intelligence of Spirit* were active in his body and that he had nothing to fear as long as this thought of divine order remained in his consciousness.

Among the first to rush to his side was a youngster whom Payne managed to ask if he happened to know a certain man living in this busy block. The boy responded by saying that he knew the man because he had often made deliveries at his apartment. The youngster dashed off with the message, and as John Payne lay there, he was persuaded that this was more than concidence. God was at work. The harmonizing, healing, adjusting power of God was taking over, and all would be well.

A chain of healing was established that included Silent Unity and Unity ministers in California and New York, but just as significant were the art and capability of skilled surgeons, Payne's fortitude and philosophy of life, his consciousness of God. When I interviewed Payne, I would never have known that the accident had ever happened to him, excepting that his faith was so tremendously secure.

That is how Unity heals.

Unity heals by the unequivocal belief that health is our heritage, that nature is remedial, that healing hands are found in many forms, medical and non-medical, that the mind is therapeutic, and that the God Spirit in man is a perfect Spirit.

Quietly creeping into the Unity movement during the 1960-1980 period was the influence of the holistic healing movement. Rising out of many sources and many needs, it was an attempt on the part of medical and allopathic practitioners to work more closely in their clinical and healing processes for the patient's good. The trend was also bringing spiritual healing, psychosomatic healing, natural healing methods through physical exercise, diet, and "therapeutic thinking" into closer relationship. Unity ministers were becoming involved, recognizing not only the potentials in this word "holism" but the sudden rise in a nation's consciousness that health is an inside job and that the "Physician within" was beginning to be recognized as a working entity for an integrated life.

Among the indications of Unity's interest in the holistic approach were articles in UNITY Magazine, repeated references to integrated living in DAILY WORD, and a co-authored book, "Healing for Everyone," by Unity's well-known minister-writer J. Sig Paulson and Dr. Evarts Loomis, a holistic-minded California physician.

A trend toward natural healing was catching on, and the power of metaphysical healing would soon be better understood in the light of *holism*. The word itself, from the Greek "holos," suggested that life is total, complete, and holy.

In Unity, all healing is divine healing. There is no conflict between science and religion. Unity admonishes individuals that if they put themselves into a doctor's hands and have confidence in the doctor, they should cooperate with the regimen proposed. If a patient harbors antagonistic feelings about the doctor, the course of healing may be blocked. Medicine, according to metaphysical teaching, is not merely a substance which produces chemical reactions, it is a thought-complex effecting results according to the relationship prevailing among the minds of the physician, the patient, and all who are involved in the healing process.

One of the most spectacular cases in which the harmony of this Unity approach was demonstrated came to my attention in St. Petersburg, Florida, when I sat with a man at a supper table. A photographer with a flash-type camera approached us with the request to take our picture. To this my companion responded somewhat whimsically, "If you are going to do that, I had better cover my eye."

When I asked him the reason for this remark, he said, "Well, you know, I have a glass eye and the light could rebound into the film!"

"A glass eye?" I asked after the photographer had gone. "I have been with you for an hour or more and I must say that I would never have noticed."

"Yes," he reflected, "it was a good surgical job."

He told me of how he had gone one day to inspect some road work for the city of St. Petersburg. As he stepped down into a pit, the iron clam-shovel suspended from a crane swung around and caught him in its fearful vice-like motion. He was lifted from the excavation before the operator was able to release the shovel and drop him to the ground. His mangled face and seemingly lifeless body made even the possibility of moving him to a stretcher or into an ambulance seem utterly futile. Nonetheless he was taken to a hospital.

By this time his wife had been notified and she in turn had called her Unity minister, Unity workers, and Silent Unity. Now she stood with the doctors during their consultation. At one point she said to the Unity minister, "I am grateful we have the best physicians possible here." The minister replied, "God, the Great Physician, is also here." The wife took her husband's hand and to the apparently unconscious form she kept repeating Unity affirmations.

In relating his story, the man said that as he lay there the words filled him with a sense of light and love. In his mind was a vision of God helping and healing, and he had no fear or doubt from that moment that he would live. Unity prayers sustained the skilled hands of the surgeons who contributed to this man's remarkable recovery. Unity affirmations gave him strength. Unity's "believability" was so strong that even today you feel it when you are with this man. His face shows few scars, but there is even less of a scar in his heart for circumstances against which he might have harbored untold resentment and bitterness.

Perhaps there will always be accidents and suffering in the world, but with faith in the *good* there is a chance, at least, that the world will evolve more toward goodness and Truth. Unity affirms that he who sees the invisible can do the impossible, and that, too, is how Unity heals. It heals by meeting situations with the interminable confidence that there is no limit to God's power.

You are God's whole and perfect child! Every cell in your body is aglow with His light, life, and love!

For developing the proper attitude toward necessary surgery, and for bringing the full force of healing faith to those who undergo hospitalization, Unity has prepared a most helpful booklet titled, "You Are Not Alone." Its thirty-three pages are spontaneous in their insight into the patient's mind, and I doubt whether more helpful material can be found than these affirmations, techniques, and inspirational hints for health. Several lines, titled "Realization," by Florence Taylor, graphically express the Unity approach:

*I can be healed. God's own life-giving power
Flows freely through my body hour by hour.*

*I must be healed so that I may express
My Father's love and joy and perfectness.*

I will be healed; for this my aim shall be,

To let God's perfect will be done in me.

I am *healed now; for just as God sees me,*
I see myself; harmonious, fearless, free.

There are endless healing affirmations in Unity. Many were composed by the Fillmores, others were inspired by Unity students or grew out of areas of need as Unity ministers went about their pastoral duties. Many were born out of the silence of Silent Unity or were submitted anonymously by individuals who had experienced extraordinary healings.

The sayings of Jesus Christ and the promise of Scripture are the rich soil from which the affirmations have grown. . . . *be transformed by the renewal of your mind* (Rom. 12:2) is at the heart of many a healing phrase. *Let this mind be in you which was also in Christ Jesus* (Phil. 2:5 A.V.) has suggested such affirmations as: *God, mighty in the midst of me, is healing my body, guiding me on my way, revealing Himself to me as my help in every need, and divine order is established in my mind, body, and affairs by the power of the indwelling Christ.*

"I am the Lord, your healer" (Exod. 15:26) gives rise to such affirmations as: *God is my strength and my peace; my heart has faith in Him. The angel of His presence guides and guards me.*

Beloved, we are God's children (I John 3:2) inspires a Unity member to say: *I am the illumined child of God, filled with the Spirit of divine love and wisdom, by which I am guided in all my ways, and led into that which is for my highest good.*

In short, every constructive Scripture text is a usable affirmation and can be transposed into a contemporary maxim which works for good. Hear the words, *"I am the light of the world,"* (John 8:12) and you can establish them in your life by affirming: *I am radiant with the light of God!*

Unity's prayer-poems also have their healing credentials. A young minister confided to me that the very first time he was called upon to pray for a desperately sick member of his congregation, he could think of no more effective words than the Prayer of Protection: *The light of God surrounds me . . .*

Among my personal investigations of so-called healing miracles in Unity, one centered around Unity's Prayer of Faith which, with its powerful affirmation, had brought about a remarkable recovery.

A woman living in a Mississippi River town

had been seized by the frightening realization that she was "slowly paralyzing." The feeling of "something holding me back" haunted her and sent her to a Minnesota hospital where her condition was diagnosed as multiple sclerosis. In her late twenties, she was adjusting herself to the role of an invalid, and her orthodox minister said it must be the will of the Lord.

One day when her husband, a civil engineer, was in a local store, a salesgirl inquired about his wife's condition.

"She's in bed," he explained. "We have engaged a nurse."

"I have something here that helped me," said the girl. "Maybe it will help her."

She handed him a Unity publication. He stuffed it into his pocket. Sheepishly he gave it to his wife. "I don't propose that what the doctors haven't been able to do, reading something is going to do," he said.

His wife paged through the booklet, read portions of it, laid it aside. The next day she picked it up again. Her eyes lingered on the Prayer of Faith: *God is my help in every need* . . .

She read it thoughtfully, put it away, read it again. The following day she memorized the stanzas and continued to repeat them slowly in quiet affirmation, especially the lines which said:

God is my health, I can't be sick;
God is my strength, unfailing, quick;
God is my all, I know no fear,
Since God and love and Truth are here.

A "feeling" came over her. Suddenly she realized she was moving her toes. Excitedly she summoned her husband and the nurse and insisted that she could walk. She was helped to her feet and took a few steps. When I visited her several weeks later she met me at the door and greeted me radiantly by saying, "I am healed."

There are spectacular and newsworthy healings in every faith, Christian and non-Christian alike, but as I stayed on at Unity Village, and when at night I saw the lighted window of Silent Unity, I realized that it is here that the unacclaimed and unpublicized therapy of prayer goes on, moment by moment and day by day. It is here that the channel for Christ's healing is kept clear through denials and affirmations, through compassion and the remedy of Truth, through holistic practice and the often inexplicable touch of the great Unknown.

The lighted window is the lighted heart, and Silent Unity is that light.

That is how Unity heals.

Its words and its voice go into lives the world around, creating the mystique that: *You are God's whole and perfect child. Every cell in your body is aglow with His light, life, and love.*

Chapter V

Of Contrasts and Continuity

Frequently, in Unity's ministerial training program, guest lecturers and teachers are invited to share areas of their spiritual research or specialties on a part-time basis. It was my privilege occasionally to present material on "World Religions," "Meditative Practices in Contemporary Faiths," and the like. During these brief 1960-1980 teaching sessions, it occurred to me that there is an intriguing contrast between those who train for the metaphysical ministry and those enrolled in traditional denominational seminaries.

One dramatic difference is that Unity Ministerial School is definitely coeducational. Another equally attractive distinction is that Unity candidates who are qualified for enrollment come from an unusual array of previous vocational backgrounds.

When I decided to study for the ministry in my parental evangelical faith, I went straight from a sheltered home and a sheltered high school to a sheltered evangelical college located on a sheltered rural campus, where the church fathers had built the school—in a walnut grove—to keep us preachers-to-be away from temptation. From this quasi-protective environment we looked forward to the day, seven years hence, when we would go out to serve a sheltered congregation.

All of us seminarians were cast in the same mold. We believed alike, had been baptised and confirmed in "our faith," completed high school, shunned the devil and most of his works, loved the Lord, and had respect, to a degree, for most of our peers. While things have changed radically since my days of ministerial indoctrination, candidates for the various Protestant ministeries, no less than for the Catholic priesthood, still represent a denominational imprint, are more or less pre-groomed for the ministry, and look upon their calling as related to the sheltering arms of Mother Church, whatever the church may be.

Societal problems rankling the secular world were decidedly remote from my seminary training. The stress and strains of people in the "labor force," their triumphs and tragedies, the vicissitudes of those who would one day be our parishioners never quite touched us in our scholarly retreat. We felt that the church was a taken-for-granted inclusion in the American system, a highly privileged, set apart institution, imminent and transcendent, like God.

We were of the opinion that "our people" were more interested in what the church stood for in the way of rituals for assuring salvation than in what we ministers could do to help them find their way to a fuller, freer life on planet Earth. We were the caretakers for their sins, thereby giving them a certain amount of freedom for additional minor sinning. There was often a lack of empathy between the people and the preacher (or priest), and a conviction persisted that a well-tempered psychological distance should be maintained between pulpit and pew.

In the classes at Unity, the situation was strikingly different. Men and women entering the Unity ministry were by no means sheltered! Nor were they cast in the same mold. Nor did they have any sanctimonious illusions about the church-at-large though they may have had some mistaken ideas about how far the historic churches had actually advanced in the past few decades.

By and large, each person who had passed the Unity ministerial admissions test had some prior career experience or accredited standing in the business world. They were a remarkably interesting mix. Of the some 200 men and women ordained by Unity during the past ten years, eighty percent had been successful in their "secular" jobs and could have continued in them but for what they felt was a call to special spiritual service.

Among a sampling in one of the classes, two students had already retired from business careers, though they were only in their late thirties. One of the women students had been a registered nurse. Another had served as administrative director of a business college. There were also a former Catholic priest, a superviser of a supermarket, a middle-aged man with military status, a woman in her late thirties whose husband had been ordained in Unity the previous year, and a musician who felt that her singing and talented song writing would stand her in good stead in Unity's "ministry through song."

These students lived, not in a dormitory, but wherever they wanted to live, some in cottages on the grounds, some commuting from surrounding towns. One couple occupied a trailer, others had apartments. All had close ties with a Unity center in their hometowns. In all cases their center leaders had recommended them to the Admissions Committee and blessed them on their way. Some were led into the ministry by reading Unity literature or by way of a healing experience. Others were inspired by their ability to straighten up a muddled life through Unity techniques. Occasionally the decision was due to a serendipitous happening or a psychic something, as of a voice or a call.

On all counts, Unity students were definitely fired up by the prospect of a career based on something empirical, on personal experiences which recognized a common bond of understanding. At this stage of the game, they were interested in divine order for the unfoldment of their lives so that they could eventually help others cope with challenges and changes comparable to their own.

They would be in training not for seven years but for two—certainly not too long for them to lose their first love. Their major subjects included: Communication Skills, Bible History and Interpretation, Truth Fundamentals, Center Operations, Counseling Practices, Prayer and Meditation—in short, practical courses for the training of ministers for the 1980s and onward.

In contrast, I recalled some of the established courses that were—and are—considered fundamental in theologically-oriented seminaries: Greek and Latin, Homiletics, Christian Ethics, Epistomology, Dogmatic

Theology, Hermeneutics, Church Doctrines, Church Rituals, Biblical Criticism, Creeds, and Catechetical Studies. In this mental print-out of these and other subjects, I could only ask myself, "What part did this learning play in my life? Where is it now? What is its relevancy in contemporary life?"

All of which prompted a closer look at Unity's educational philosophy. Its purpose is focused on teaching the reality of the activity of God in human life. Its curriculum deals with Truth Fundamentals, Prayer Techniques, Healing Meetings, Communication, Counseling, Creative Programming, Youth Education, and Meditative Workshops.

I can speak only of my impression about the avid interest of these trainees as they responded to my courses in contemporary religions of the world. I can only conclude that the ministry, for them, will not revolve around a theological Sunday affair, a dialectic about creeds and canons of the past, but about a ministry in a workaday world among a visible and invisible fellowship at the point where the worshiper or the seeker lives. Those who affirm this kind of vocation must unmistakably represent one reason for Unity's success in the spiritual life stream of our time.

The environment in which this ministerial training takes place is another point of special interest. Explain consciousness however you wish or describe a "collective unconscious" however you will (Fillmore called it the "sense mind of the human race"), there is definitely a mystical power that has been generated through the years here at Unity headquarters. The time is coming when there will be Unity ministerial training centers in other locations, in other parts of America, but here at the fountainhead, wellsprings of commitment run deep. For the sheer adventure of the spirit of Unity, this is the place!

The influence of the Fillmore founders needs no further credential than the fact that their lives and writings represent the truths and textuary as Charles and Myrtle established them. These cofounders were sufficiently open-ended to permit continual examination of whatever else in the way of canonical or apocryphal insight the broad field of metaphysics had to offer.

Lowell and Rickert Fillmore contributed immeasurably to the mystique that plays such a vital role in the Unity story. Rick's passing in 1965 at the age of eighty-one, creatively active to the very time of his death, and Lowell's transition in 1975 in his ninety-fourth year of an inspiringly dedicated and productive life put imperishable imprints on the continuity of the mystique.

I would imagine that the closeness to the presence of Lowell and Rick would also give students and visitors at Unity headquarters a feeling of intimacy. A year before Rick's passing, I stood on the tower with him as I had in the 1940s. He was still the tall, compelling, deep-thinking man who lived determinedly in two worlds at once, the world of structured things and the world of creativity. Fully at home in each, he evidently had unseen helpers who were as real to him as mutual friends, and no doubt he saw cosmic trails as clearly as he saw the paths that wound through the Unity grounds.

When I commented on how the world continued to press in on Unity Village, how the highways were widening and the tower stood changeless in the midst of change, Rick remarked, "Father said it was to be the fulfillment of prophecy."

Years ago he had told me the same thing, but now he added, "You are not going to get people to be exclusive about religion when science and cultures and world situations are reminding us of the need for understanding the unity of the whole cosmic plan." These were the days of the ecumenical movement, and it was part of Rick's Emersonian thinking when he suggested, "There is no true religion without freedom and no freedom without true faith."

It is this pervading *mystical consciousness* that makes Unity great, and the fact must be noted and included in the secrets of Unity's appeal. The mystique has also emanated from dedicated Unity workers whose influence they themselves may never quite realize. It has been generated by staff members and officials, by ministers in the field, and by departmental heads whose lives and contributions have been made selflessly and without thought of gain.

What we are talking about here is a transhumanized state of experience not self-imposed but spiritually prompted. It is not any claim to cosmic consciousness or messianic illusion but simply an inner awakening or special nearness to God. I have a hunch that these experiences, collectively, leave a layer or layers of light that are seen or felt by people sensitive to such phenomena. It is more than something merely auric or psychic. It is the awareness that there are lighted lives just as there are lighted windows, and there are bearers of the light as well. Which is to say that what I have called "mystical consciousness" or the "mystique" is for real, an illumination that remains, as far as I am concerned, basic in Unity.

During my Unity research I often ask people at Unity retreats and Unity centers, "What have you found in Unity?" The results consistently included the answer, "A religion that can be lived."

This was stated in various ways:

An honesty about religion.

A teaching that makes sense.

A new challenge.

Prosperity.

The inspiration of DAILY WORD.

The power of prayer.

Practical teachings.

A wonderful Sunday school for my children.

No talk about sin and punishment.

A happy religion.

A God of love.

Creative power of thought and words.

The meaning of prayer.

Great fellowship.

The real meaning of Jesus Christ.

Inner balance.

Physical healing.

An honesty about life after death.

Frequently there was the answer, "An

honesty about life after death." And in Unity's ministerial training, the teaching covers not only the activity of God in every phase of *life* but in life after life as well.

How thinking and discussion on this subject were changing in the public mind during the 1960-1980 periods was evident in a growing interest in reincarnation, seminars and lectures on life before life, life after life, questions on when is a person truly dead, thanatology, eternalism, life-extension, death: a new state of consciousness.

I told a group of students and retreatants at a Unity Village get-together that an instructor in creative writing once said to me, "Never write about anything morbid, like death or dying. In the first place nobody knows anything about it except those who have experienced it, and they won't tell; and secondly, nobody wants to read about dying because they don't believe it will happen to them anyway."

We agreed that a dramatic change had taken place in our thinking since the outspoken professor laid down this dictum. People *are* interested in what happens after death, and futhermore, the subject need not be morbid. If we go to a strange country, shouldn't we find out something about it before we make the trip, learn a bit about its life and customs? People are asking more questions about life's continuum than ever before, part of which may be due to the precariousness of the world in which we live and the feeling that one false or foolish click of a button could joust us into that other world in less time than it takes to tell.

I mentioned that wherever I went in my lecture work, whether to college campuses or religious conferences, the topic of life after death was always high on the agenda, and I recognized that men and women of Unity have answers which would be helpful to other groups.

My investigation of so-called mediums came into the discussion, and I confessed that my experiences included the meaningful and the meaningless, the genuine and the faked, the evidential and the questionable, all of which are part of the vast arc of research in this intriguing field.

Growing in popularity in the 1970s was the research in death and dying conducted by Dr. Elisabeth Kubler-Ross. A Swiss-born medical doctor, Kubler-Ross shared an interest in my research and I in hers. We had many interchanges of ideas and agreed that life's metamorphosis has no better symbol in nature than the butterfly which the ancient Greeks referred to as the "psyche." This had interesting connotations in a metaphysical context.

As we talked about these things in front of the open fireplace—fireless on a balmy Friday night—and helped ourselves to snacks and fruit of various kinds, it was always easy to come back to the words, "Live now! Live fully!" But throughout the range of history and religious lore, death and dying have forever been the most mysterious and inexplicable occurrences in life's inescapable encounters.

Charles Fillmore was interested in spiritualism at an early stage in his questing, but he dropped it abruptly and warned against it. While he felt that there were valid psychic phenomena, he saw no reason to depend on discarnate spirit guidance and look to mediums for help when the God Presence is available. And why seek to prove that death does not end all when Jesus Christ had already conclusively validated that Truth?

Furthermore, Fillmore contended, since we have access to the Spirit of Jesus Christ and to the Christ Mind, why not spend the time in developing *this* connection? Thus persuaded, he warned Truth seekers to stay away from spiritualism. *We teach spiritual Truth,* he proclaimed, *and Truth and spiritualism are as wide apart as the poles.*

His major contribution in the area of life after life was twofold: God did not create man to die, and reincarnation is a subject worthy of serious consideration. I was eager to discuss these points with the group, but they wanted me to define the position of the institutionalized church on the subject of life after death. This was fair enough, but I had to submit that Christian opinions about immortality vary all the way from belief in an instantaneous, miraculous transport of the soul to God's throne of judgment, to the theory that the dead remain somberly in their graves until some specially appointed resurrection morn. The average Protestant would likely be hard put to articulate the church's deepest convictions about the world beyond.

Hell is definitely "out" as far as liberal protestantism is concerned, and heaven is being redefined, just as Catholicism is reappraising purgatory and as fundamentalism is compelled to reevaluate, in the light of science, many notions it once irrevocably held about the Promised Land.

Surely, I had to say, heaven and hell are now spiritually interpreted by the church-at-large as states of consciousness, and not as geographic locations. Heaven and hell are areas of awareness in which the soul or psyche continues its development nearer to the reality of God than was possible on this physical plane. Golden streets, heavenly thrones, harps and halos, no less than alabaster stairs and wings for flying are fantasies of the past or valid symbols for metaphysical interpretations. The "many mansions" are no longer etheric condominiums but, according to modern theology, states of mind or being. This, it occurred to me, comes startlingly close to Unity's original idea when, in one of his bold declarations, Charles Fillmore said: *We believe all the doctrines of Christianity* spiritually interpreted!

"What about final judgment?" one of the young men wanted to know, saying that he and a fundamentalist had been discussing the subject.

I submitted that the institutionalized church still generally insisted on a divine reckoning of some kind, but the nature of this judgment was also being rethought in ecclesiastical circles. While degrees of "punishment and rewards" are still basic in the church's thinking, there is now a good deal of uncertainty about how delicate the scale is attuned on which one's virtues and vices will be weighed. Persisting in Christian thought is the redemptive work of Jesus Christ, but there are those who now believe with Unity that: *Through conscious union with Jesus in the regeneration, one can transform one's body and make it perpetually healthy, therefore immortal, and in this way attain eternal life.*

A new age of thought about Judgment Day was definitely being ushered in, and what lay beyond that judgment was something more than the orthodox concept of heaven or hell had ever satisfied.

So, now, what was Unity's answer to this ultimate, all-pervading question? And what about the intriguing supposition that God never intended that we should *ever* die?

A Friday night seemed an appropriate time for our discussion, and in this friendly room I tried to synthesize, on the basis of student interest and belief, what *Unity* believes and what Unity proclaims about death and dying.

First of all, Unity believes in reincarnation, but in a way that must be carefully explained. A generally accepted meaning of reincarnation is the belief that the essence of life, our life force, returns to express itself after death in another time, another place, and another body, until it finally gains divine perfection and lives eternally—for God never intended that we should die.

Charles Fillmore, with blunt courage, once declared: *The Western world in general looks upon reincarnation as a heathen doctrine. Many persons close the door of their mind upon it without waiting to find out what message it brings when interpreted in the light of Truth.*

He then interpreted it. He saw reincarnation as a process leading toward eternal life in a manner not unlike that proposed by the great religions of the East. In all of these religions is the hint that we must be born again and again because we have not yet learned how to *live*. When we learn how to live, we will cease learning how to die. In other words, when we learn how to live to our utmost spiritual capacity, we will live forever, and reincarnation will have served its purpose.

When Fillmore was accused of being somewhat heathenistic in his own thinking, he replied: *Through the light of the indwelling Christ the so-called heathen have discerned many truths to which the more material-minded people of newer countries have been blind. Whenever there has been a nation of thinkers who were not bound in materialism, those thinkers have accepted reincarnation as*

*a fact. It is rejected only where the craze for
wealth and for fame and for the things of the
world has darkened the mind with materiality.*

"But how does reincarnation work?" I
asked the group.

"It is like putting a new light bulb in place
of one that has burned out," one of the men
suggested. "The power of God is the circuit."

"Death is actually a process of birth," said
a young woman.

"Reincarnation is simply part of the total
life cycle," said another. "There are many
states of consciousness."

Differences between Unity's belief in reincarnation and Hindu and Buddhist beliefs
were thoroughly aired in our evening rendezvous. For one thing—and quite obviously—Unity never believed, as some Hindu
groups do, in transmigration of souls, by
which is meant the retrogression of souls into
lower states of existence. Nor was reincarnation interpreted in a strictly Eastern sense.
To Eastern, non-Christian groups, reincarnation is an evolutionary process, a chain of
cause and effect. To Unity, it is a "unifying
force" through which God seeks to restore us
to our original deathless state.

In this connection, interestingly enough,

Unity believes that death came into the world through the Adamic man, and this resulted in body dissolution. But in the demonstration of the overcoming of death, as shown in the Resurrection of Jesus Christ, the restoration of the "lost Eden" is already begun.

To the Hindu and Buddhist, reincarnation is inseparable from the law of karma, which is the ethical consequence of the process of cause and effect. The Hindu carries with him the result of his previous acts and is tied, in a very real sense, to karmic law. His life is the net result of his conduct in previous existence. Fillmore referred to the Hindu as *a weary treadmill traveler from birth to death and from death to birth*. I suggested that Hindus and Buddhists would not agree with this concept, but Fillmore, even as Albert Schweitzer, saw Hinduism as a philosophy of life negation and Christianity as a process of life affirmation.

Fillmore contended: *Through repeated trials at living, man is discovering that he must learn to control the issues of life. Divine law, as taught by Jesus, must be understood and applied to all life's details, and when this is done, the "Eden state" will be restored and man will live forever.*

A member of the group had an interesting

observation. "Is it possible," he wondered, "that Mr. Fillmore might have been thinking also in terms of life expectancy, and could he perhaps have been quite right in his assumption that if we learn how to live properly, we *may* live forever? After all, life expectancy has been steadily rising. A child born these days may expect to live to be seventy or eighty or even a hundred. In Papa Charley's day, life expectancy was only fifty. If each generation can add ten or fifteen years to the span of life, given time, we will be living awfully long! If we add spiritual know-how to physical know-how, inasmuch as the body is, after all, a single unit, perhaps we can reach a state where we will never die."

Another participant had an equally provocative theory. She proposed that because Eastern people do not have our creature comforts and conveniences, they do not have our "will to live" and consequently occupy themselves more with thoughts of dying. We, *enjoying* our way of life, are more inclined to think in terms of living! "Dying," she proposed, "is therefore more unpopular in the Western world than it is in the East."

In its perspective of the life stream, Unity looked upon death as the great negation which will one day be overcome. It is a phenomenon that should neither be feared nor welcomed. It is a neutral state, progressive only as we learn that it can eventually lead to a full knowledge of spiritual union with God. The key thought in Unity remains: God did not intend that we should die. But because of the present *fact* of death, Unity accepts it as it does many other facts, the fact of sickness, for example, or poverty or darkness. They are facts, not Truth, and each will be vanquished in its time—sickness by the Truth of health, poverty by the Truth of substance, darkness by the Truth of light, and finally death by the Truth of life.

We concluded that death is a rest period preparing us for an awakening to another day of adventure. Death is that part of life that prepares a person for more and greater living. Death is an error of mind. In fact, in Unity death is not death, it is *transition.* It is not the end of consciousness but a change in consciousness.

There is no room in the Unity eschatalogical system for a heaven filled with busybody souls living a "spiritually suburban" kind of life. Fillmore contended such an idea of heaven was created by mortal mind which sought to perpetuate *all the old family relationships as man knows them in his present life.*

Personal consciousness is insufficient to demonstrate eternal life, Fillmore insisted. *The great family of Christ, the whole redeemed Adam race is all* one, *and the little selfish relationships of the Adam man have no place in the new order.*

Heaven, true heaven, can only be a kingdom in which *all* of us have learned how to live. Heaven must of necessity be incomplete unless all people have overcome death. It is logically true that in any real heaven, spiritual kinship will be more important than family relationships, and in heaven, the consciousness of all humankind will need to approximate the consciousness of God.

While such conclusions seemed to me comparable to the Nirvanic state described in Hinduism and Buddhism, the Unity group would not carry the analogy that far. Unity's main basis of agreement with Eastern religions lay in the fact that reincarnation provides the most equitable plan for the total understanding of life.

Surely a just and righteous God would see to it that every soul has repeated and equal opportunities to work out its salvation. A deformed child, a premature death, a sudden tragedy, all of these, no less than the young

250

genius, the gifted prodigy, the talented mind—each has a meaning and each is an argument for reincarnation.

"A single span of life," Unity insists, "does not constitute one's entire opportunity for life."

Judging from our evening seminar, most Unity students affirm that Unity is more interested in life here and now than in the hereafter. Which reminded me that in my research among the many religions of the world, few brought the spirit of living as fully into the total spectrum of life as Unity.

You realize this at Unity's memorial services. They are devoid of morbidity and shorn of doleful hymns or funeral eulogies. There are none of the "ashes to ashes, dust to dust" references or reminders of the well-worn phrase, "when worms destroy this body," and no macabre viewing of the body of the departed. In Unity, where cremation is the general rule, the service emphasizes the beauty and serenity of life, together with God's good in the living of it.

As to grief and mourning, these, too, are brought into a new perspective. After our meeting a student referred me to an article by William A. Clough in which, with typical Unity approach, the persuasive thesis is pro-

251

claimed that:

Grief is not a sign of weakness, for the greatest men have known deep grief. But they have manifested their greatness by rising above and overcoming their grief by claiming the joy that is their rightful heritage. Grief is human; joy is divine.

Grief is part of human nature, but joy is part of our divine nature ... Prolonged mourning may be an indication of too great a self-concern. We are mourning then not for the one who has gone, but for ourselves. When the letter "u" is taken from the word mourning, *the word becomes* morning, *the dawn of a new day!*

Contrasting this point of view with the customary reflection on death, we realize again that Unity is not interested in conforming to ancient presuppositions but is eager to explore new approaches to life's confrontations. I suppose a person can better show love for someone by adjusting to life than by bemoaning death, and I thought again that there is probably no better way of demonstrating one's faith than by the constant reminder that, though death is truly a fact, it is *not* a fact in *Truth.*

After our good-nights were said, I went for a walk through the Unity grounds, asking myself how often men and women have speculated on immortality in closed rooms, only to find their assurance of it under the starlit sky. I found such assurances as I walked alone. I sensed it in the night sounds, felt it in the hush of Unity Village, and was reminded of it whenever I saw the lighted window and the tower.

Surely there is an unbroken line of questing souls in all faiths everywhere in the world who keep the hope of immortality alive by their knowledge that God is life, that all is life, and that life is God. But this, I realized anew, requires faith, and faith requires reflection.

I understood Charles Fillmore better just now than ever before. I understood what he meant when he said that perhaps he would never die. He may have meant this quite literally, having foreseen for himself what some modern scientists are now predicting for people of the future: a scientific breakthrough which, together with our ever-increasing knowledge about the nature of life, will make the saying a physical reality: God did not intend that we should ever die.

As the stars looked down over Unity Village it occurred to me that Charles and Myrtle Fillmore may very well have been right in their theory but wrong in their calculation.

It was Myrtle who said: *Jesus Christ promised repeatedly that those who believe firmly enough should never see death, and we also believe this to be true. Death has no part in God's eternal plan.*

Some day, as the centuries turn, it will happen. Through someone, somewhere, believing firmly enough, Truth will be demonstrated. And who is to say who that someone is or who that someone will be?

Right in theory but wrong in calculation. Is this not often true of those who, by a destiny beyond their knowing, live, as if by divine appointment, ahead of their time?

Part Three

Perspective on the Future

(1980s to 21st Century)

Chapter I

Unity's Role in the World

By the 1980s metaphysical thinking had broken into traditional churches of practically all denominations, first as a thief in the night, and then as an invited guest urged to stay.

Whenever I attended services or participated in the activities of liberal, evangelical churches, I realized how their emphases were shifting from traditional theology to "modern metaphysics." Concepts of the "indwelling Christ," use of affirmations, frequent references to metaphysical phrases, such as *expect a miracle, divine order, universal mind, creative power of mind,* and *I am one with God* were becoming part of religion's vernacular and of the life of its people as well. The winds of change were moving through American churches and through society-at-large.

Unity, as we have seen, had quietly set ecclesiastical doors ajar by the unsolicited endorsements of Protestant clergy who shared the teachings with their people on the basis of practical contemporary appeal. Unity literature persistently found its way into the tributaries of almost all Christian denominations, and it was now becoming ever more recognizable in the mainstream of our nation's spiritual life.

A graphic analogy bearing on all this came to mind one day when I was jotting down notes about Unity in our cabin on Kootenay Lake in British Columbia. From my study window, the four-mile wide, hundred-mile long expanse of water seemed to stretch out into infinity. Flowing through Kootenay Lake was the Kootenay River which gave the lake its name, its lively blue color, and its substance. This river, which has never been accurately measured, is part of the lake, and the lake is part of the river. The river is deep, silent, and uncommonly strong. You might say it is also invisible until you get into it and feel its current. It nourishes the lake, and the lake with its many mountain streams nourishes the river. It is all reciprocal.

If you imagine the lake to be America, then the river is Unity—silent, unmeasurable, nourishing and being nourished as it flows steadily through the shifting moods of our nation's life. Who is to measure its influence? Who is to say this is where Unity ends and there is where Christianity or any religious expression begins? Like the lake and the river, it is reflexive, and you can see the analogy from your own study window, if you will.

It can be seen even clearer if we get out of the study and go to Unity centers where the action is, and to Unity headquarters which is the axis of the action and the fountainhead of the Unity stream. It is then that the analogy becomes real, especially if viewed against the exciting paradox of the 1980s. Everything from national politics to international affairs was in dramatic transition at the dawn of 1980. The value of things we live by were in flux, from money to morals and religion.

The obvious first part of the religious paradox was this: Not only had modern metaphysics been accepted by the churches but there was tremendous interest among non-churched people in the adventure Unity calls "applied Christianity." This interest had always been true to a degree, but it was "truer" now. Concern for a new security in life and an emphasis not on the past but very much on the present, with a wistful glance toward the dawn of the 21st century, were part of the new order. People were on their own secret quests, and many had long ago given up on the traditionalism and literalism of the "old time religion." Now, because of a growing need for order and balance in their lives, no less than a deepened awareness of their relationship with *all* life, they interpreted the term *spiritual* as extending far beyond an institutionalized faith. In fact, the word *religion* itself had become too restrictive to express the total search for Truth.

In these opening 1980s, the search for meaning was talked about as a coded-in, innate impulse to believe in a workable, provable, meaningful God, active in one's daily affairs. The spiritual drive was now an inner journey as natural and instinctive as love, sex, self-preservation, or the will to live. All of this constituted one side of the paradox of the 1980s and was construed by many as part of the phenomenon of modern metaphysics. Unity was one of its strongest advocates.

On the other side of the paradoxical equation was what might be called *theological metaphysics*. This, too, carried a strong attraction. In fact, the media and the movies were giving it prime time and attention as if it might provide religion's ultimate answer. It not only assured salvation but also an escape from frustration, and it warned an often jittery world that a not-to-be-fooled-with God was still in charge of things. Theological metaphysics had strong political implications—clout. It was morally *right* and righteous. It championed the need for the baptism of the Holy Ghost and the "gut feeling" (as one advocate put it) of "being saved." It was Pentecostal. It was fundamental. I knew it well. I experienced it all and was in the midst of it for at least two full years with the Assembly of God people. Baptism, glossolalia, the fervor, and the passion of "born again," Armageddon concepts had been mine. Its tongues were *as of fire* (Acts 2:3), and its spirit that of a *rush of mighty wind.* (Acts 2:2)

Closely related and TV conscious were the ultra modern seers and prophets of the *theological metaphysics* crusade. They were prophets of hope *and* doom, of mercy *and* condemnation. They were raising billions of dollars to save the starving people of the world, to help the needy, to send Bibles to communistic countries, and to "save all sinners." They were sentencing those to damnation who refused to accept Jesus *now*. They were dispatching camera crews to foreign lands to prove that the lost *were* being saved in the very presence of the camera's eye. They had God's timetable for the end of the world. Their apocalyptic coverage ranged from the coming of an old-fashioned end-of-the-world to planetary wars with nuclear annihilation imaged in the public mind.

Hadn't these modern soothsayers and seers ever heard of Unity? Hadn't they ever been told about Unity's earliest days a century ago? Didn't they know that in the *1880s* the same kind of ghoulish predictions were in vogue, voiced by their own counterparts who also had God's timetable figured out just as accurately a hundred years ago?

In those days, when Charles and Myrtle Fillmore were facing their tests of faith, people were told that the Horses of the Apocalypse were being unleashed to trample America to certain death. Yet somehow the Fillmores and other modern metaphysicians in their time *denied* the prophecy and *affirmed* that the horses would be turned around and driven back by the power of Mind and the action of a God of love and Truth. But this time, in the awesome 1980s, we were assured that it was not America alone that would be trampled but the world.

In the midst of the paradox, Unity was growing. It was growing if for no reason than that it was an open-ended faith designed to keep one's life and spiritual thought unswerving from the goal that *God is good.* It was growing because, as Fillmore had foreseen: *The great need of the whole human family is to know that the one supreme law of God as Spirit is manifesting itself in the mind of man.*

Unity could not by any logic or contrivance ascribe to God a lower morality or sensitivity than we human beings possess. "The innermost *you*," Unity was saying, "is God's expression made in His own image and likeness. Do not settle for anything less. Do not dwell on anything lower. Because God is Spirit, you, too, are Spirit. Your purpose in life is to realize yourself as divine so that you may become a child of God in actuality."

Unity was in a strategic position during this paradoxical period. It had always been Christ-centered, Christ-oriented. What it called its "basic principle" was a return to the Truth that the life that Jesus Christ lived is the kind of life toward which we, as children of God, should earnestly strive and to which we, in fact, are heirs.

Who in Christendom, on whichever side of the paradox, could disagree? Who, open to the spiritual quest, would be unwilling to accept the meaning of such a principle?

Unity was on solid ground metaphysically

and theologically, and it was growing as a sign of hope in the midst of these utterly incongrous "last days" predicted for the '80s.

I saw Unity's contemporary growth firsthand, for I was deeply involved in workshops and seminars in the modern metaphysical field. Or for the sake of the analogy of the Kootenay River, let me say that I was working in the "lake land" of America's religious faiths through which the Unity stream was flowing.

The 1980s were destined to present precisely the challenges that modern metaphysics needed to test its tensile strength, challenges that faced all "Truth movements." In fact, they faced all religions. Worldwide, the very foundations of institutionalized faiths—Christian, non-Christian, religions ancient and contemporary—were being tested as seldom before.

The 1980s were bluntly asking whether traditional beliefs out of which the meaning had gone should be perpetuated. What were the traditional clergy's honest views on such issues as sin, salvation, the Ten Commandments, suffering, racial equality, sexual equality, matters of morality, and matters of life and death? People wanted to know how much longer religious strife could continue.

In simple terms, here were religions of the world at war among themselves, between themselves, and giving the impression of holding to the rationale that God is on the side of those who have the greatest weapons. The battle of Armageddon, to those who had eyes to see and hearts to listen, was being fought in the minds of humanity. The real conflict was in the deep longing of the Spirit of Truth and its frustrated capacity for love and peace.

Unity was growing. Though the kingdom cometh not by observation, as the saying goes, it could not go unnoticed that there were now more than 300 Unity centers stretching from the American mainland to Alaska, Hawaii, and "beyond North America" to so many distant points that an Overseas department had been established at Unity headquarters to coordinate this global outreach.

The Unity ministries were banded together under the Association of Unity Churches (AUC). It was responsible for examining, training, ordaining, and placing Unity ministers.

Wherever I went I found evidence of AUC's advancing program. It could be seen in bigger churches than we customarily associated with the Unity movement, functional churches with educational, recreational, and spiritual growth facilities; churches with rooms for counseling, biofeedback training, audio-visual teaching programs, prayer chapels, literature and library departments, and excellent Sunday school facilities. Many emphasized Unity youth and Unity educational advance training, including Montessori methods and the Wilhelm School for the development of new earth children for a new age.

The physical facilities of Unity centers gave indication that here was long-range planning with a spiritual, educational emphasis on the fact that the challenges of the 1980s had to be met most of all on the personal front. I had the feeling that Unity ministers were still more interested in getting their life-changing "Truth work" across than they were in membership campaigns or any kind of "evangelization." At the same time, however, center affiliation and the attendance records were gradually becoming a gauge of growth, and signs of a token measure of success. So were the building programs. If traditional Christian churches were copying Unity philosophy, AUC was turning eyes to traditional builders of modern religious empires such as Dr. Robert Schuller was demonstrating in his Crystal Cathedral in Garden Grove, California. For AUC's 1981 conference, Schuller was asked to speak. After all, here was an orthodox minister who had created a multi-million dollar work and attracted a million followers.

I recalled a Sunday morning in the 1970s when I was speaking for Michael Murphy, minister at Hawaii's Unity Church on Diamond Head. Dr. Schuller attended the first of three services, this one at 7:30 a.m. When we shook hands at the door, he tarried to assure me how much Unity principles meant to him and how helpful they had been to him in his work. So his coming to AUC was reciprocal, and how interesting indeed, in terms of our analogy, to try to separate the many religious rivers from the spiritual lakes of life!

A Lutheran minister, a longtime friend of mine who dropped in at Unity Church of Christianity in Houston during my assignment there, was overpowered by what was going on in "this thing called Unity." He made no pretense of hiding his bewilderment that this booming church was built in the shape of a pyramid. Pyramid-power, he insisted, belonged more to the occult than to Christianity.

"And furthermore as to Unity," he quipped, "what are they doing about the *Great Commission?*"

The Great Commission! The term came back to me as a voice out of the past. The Great Commission had nothing to do with money or with the uncertain economic state of things. Or perhaps it did, for in Christian theological circles it came straight out of Matthew 28:18. To traditional ministers, including myself, the text had always been interpreted as God's marching orders:

And Jesus came and said to them, "Go, therefore . . . and make disciples of all nations, baptizing them in the name of the Father and of the Son and of the Holy Spirit, teaching them to observe all that I have commanded you. . . . "

My friend's question carried the obvious implication, "Where are the Unity *missionaries*? Why aren't they stationed around the world baptizing new converts and saving the 'unsaved'?"

Yet, even in Lutheranism, which had once sounded the trumphet blast of the Reformation, the evidence of an appreciation for metaphysical thought could be found in this Lutheran pastor. As we talked about the history of Protestantism with its many tributaries, even he was willing to consider that perhaps baptism *could* be a *symbolic* cleansing of heart and mind, and that just by chance, the Bible and Jesus Christ's teachings might at times be interpreted on a deeper than literal basis. Wasn't it the inner meaning that Jesus was emphasizing when He used outer symbols, parables, and axioms rich in Truth? Hadn't Unity, as a living faith, built its entire structure on the concept of "teaching" as the Great Commission advised? And aren't there ways to send the Word into all the world without going there in person?

Which reminded me that DAILY WORD had now reached a global readership of 2 million, and who could guess how many more readers besides the subscribers were being benefited and getting a message and "finding God" and being baptized not with water but in Spirit and in Truth?

It is no secret, nor is it necessarily news, that DAILY WORD has had a place in the White House ever since Eisenhower days. Each president in turn has been familiar with it. The Kennedys read it. I personally gave Lyndon Johnson a copy when I met him in Texas during my escorting of a Japanese religious delegation across the country.

Two prominent Unity ministers, J. Sig Paulson and William L. Fischer, gave the opening prayers at sessions of the House of Representatives in Washington, D.C. in the early 1980s. Chaplains for a day, their prayers and their presence were in the tradition of Unity's respect for the sanctity of America's concept of unity in diversity. Earlier, Grace Free, minister of Unity Church of Christ in Hammond, Indiana, had been accorded the same honor. Prayers for "Government and Country" are recorded in the Congressional Record, and there it is noted that Rev. Free was chaplain on three occasions, in 1972, 1975, and 1978. Grace shared with me the interesting footnote that at one of these sessions she had personal meetings with both Gerald Ford and Thomas (Tip) O'Neill, Jr. Unity was by no means as popular then as now, and women ministers were still on probation. Grace was definitely a breakthrough figure.

Now, radio and TV appearances were part of the onward going programs featuring Unity leaders across the country. In New York, at Unity Center of Practical Christianity, Eric Butterworth was setting a productive pace in audiovisual programming and inspiring others to follow in a modern "teaching ministry." In Florida, Astronaut Edgar D. Mitchell was on the teaching staff of Unity of the Palm Beaches. In California, a Unity minister was in his second year of hosting a daily half-hour TV program, "There Is a Way," interviewing representatives of Unity, the International New Thought Alliance, and ministers of many faiths.

Let there be Unity! Unity playing its role in the world of faiths. Unity that demonstrates the power of conviction.

Let there be Unity. Unity that will never become rigidly denominationalized. Unity that remains a living, loving faith, combining beauty and art with the electrical charge of a living light. Unity that makes children of us all and masters of our fate.

Those were some of the enthusiastic impressions I jotted down as my assignments crisscrossed not only Unity centers but denominational churches and college campuses. My notes were full of impressions in these opening 1980 periods: *Paths of understanding are becoming ever closer and more meaningful. All roads that lead to God are good. Religions have more in common than in conflict. God is Spirit eternal; Spirit is life immortal; life is Mind universal. We are entering a new era and a new age.*

I also jotted down any number of questions, such as: Why are there so many liberal-minded Christians and liberal, freethinking members of the Jewish faith joining Unity? Why, when their own churches are themselves turning more and more to modern metaphysical teachings?

Again, DAILY WORD provided an answer. This inspirational faith builder was consistently holding back the tides of doom with its positive, authoritative philosophy of the good, the true, the beautiful. Silent Unity was another reason. Unique among religions, it rarely failed to do some special good or work some "miracle." Like DAILY WORD, it refused to see or admit the paradox. Instead, it held to its constant continuity that all people are God's children, all faiths are part of God's holy family. It told everyone everywhere, "The prayers of Silent Unity can help you to know the power of God within you and within all persons. They can be like a bridge over which you walk from fear to faith. Call on Silent Unity for prayers for yourself or another. Write to Silent Unity, Unity Village, Missouri, 64065. Call Silent Unity 816-251-2100 any time day or night. If you have an urgent need and have no means of paying for the call, you may call toll-free. The number is 800-821-2935."

There was another reason for members coming into Unity from the "established" faiths, and from the unchurched field, and from both sides of the paradox. The Unity ministers and their staffs were microcosms of DAILY WORD and Silent Unity. Modern metaphysics was becoming a practical working tool in creating hopeful, healthy, helpful living. Unity centers had a freshness, a free-wheeling, free-flowing spirit of comaraderie. Five minutes into a Unity service, as I have often said, you are in a heightened state of consciousness. It is part of the mystique, and it is an inside job. Unity is a feeling religion.

Older Christian religions, religions that date back to church fathers and reformers, are intellectually skilled in theological metaphysics based on what is called "pure reason." Unity is skilled in modern metaphysical theology embracing scientific, psychological, and psychoanalytical reasoning. In its training and its aspirations to knowledge, Unity has not forgotten an important footnote to the quest, "I don't care how much you know, I want to know how much you care."

Theological metaphysics presents a thesis of sinful man—and woman—and a plan of salvation focused on a literal heaven, a literal hell, and a Bible to be taken literally. Modern metaphysics suggests the concept of a sinless child of God, the Christ Spirit incarnated, a plan of salvation focused on heaven and hell as states of consciousness here and now no less than in the hereafter, and on a Bible to be taken both literally and symbolically.

Theological metaphysics goes back to the scholastics in the Middle Ages and is a system of logic. Modern metaphysics goes back to pre-Christian Aristotelians and is a system involving philosophy, science, and religion.

Theological metaphysics sees God's plan as being foreordained or at least foreknown. Modern metaphysics sees it as unfolding according to cause and effect and divine principles and laws.

Theological metaphysics "salutes the Christ in *me*." Modern metaphysics "salutes the Christ in *you*" because the Christ in me is God's universal Christ known by many names in many ways and places.

Most religions, sensitive to modern life and times, reflect a feeling of caring and sharing in their services. This is particularly true in Unity. Its affirmations, prayers, meditations, the offering, and the lesson (sermon) are strongly personalized. Idealistically, every person becomes an "individualized center of God-consciousness" with the assurance that God's mind and God's power are ever available through the realization of this personalization. Since the individual is one with God, every person is one with every other person. Humanity itself is an expression of God as creative force in the universe, and all is in divine order. The paradox has been resolved and all is well.

There is a revealing insight into Unity's personalization and outlook on life in the songs used at the Sunday services. Lovable old-time hymns such as "Rock of Ages" or "Abide with Me" have melodies that are immortal. The music for these is public domain, but many of the words that accompany these melodies are of such another age of thought, of mood and direction, that they had to go. Or at least they had to be reconsidered in the light of new thinking about God and His creation and the love and joy of faith. So new verses written by metaphysically-minded authors were substituted, demonstrating how consciousness is kept contemporary while still wedded to the undying music of the past.

ROCK OF AGES (traditional)
Rock of Ages, cleft for me,
Let me hide myself in thee;
Let the water and the blood
From Thy riven side which flowed,
Be of sin the double cure,
Save me from its guilt and power.

Not the labors of my hands
Can fulfill Thy law's demands;
Could my zeal no respite known,
Could my tears forever flow,
All for sin could not atone;
Thou must save, and Thou alone.

ROCK OF AGES (Unity)
Rock of Ages, Truth divine,
Strong foundation, ever mine;
Safe, secure, I here remain;
In the peace He doth ordain;
Living ever in the light,
Pure and perfect in God's sight.

On the rock of Truth I stand,
Destiny at my command;
Filled with peace and pow'r of God,
Boundless good, eternal love;
Safe with Truth, so firm and strong,
Praising in triumphant song.

ABIDE WITH ME (traditional)
Abide with me!
fast falls the evening tide;
The darkness deepens,
Lord with me abide!
When other helpers fail;
and comforts flee;
Help of the helpless,
O abide with me!

Swift to its close
ebbs out life's little day;
Earth's joy grow dim,
its glories pass away;
Change and decay
in all around I see;
O Thou, who changest not,
abide with me!

ABIDE WITH ME (Unity)
Abide with me,
the dawn of day is here;
Darkness has vanished,
light is shining clear;
Truth's glorious message
makes the glad earth free;
O holy Comforter,
abide with me!

I need Thy presence,
satisfying, pure,
All else is changing,
Thou alone art sure.
Who, like Thyself,
my guide and stay can be?
Thru joy eternal,
Lord, abide with me.

I caught something of the application of Unity's philosophy long ago when I visited with music master Carl Frangkiser. This highly skilled musician, disillusioned with institutionalized religion and disquieted by the way of the world, turned his back on any attempt to figure out things "religiously." After a period of military service, he came out of the army with a questing spirit. When he heard of Unity he was persuaded that this approach to faith was what he needed and wanted. Offering his services to the Unity cause, he composed many Unity hymns, some adapted to lyrics written by Unity ministers. An offertory, with words by Francis J. Gable, gives a good idea of the Unity point of view:

I give my offering to God
Because He gives to me.

I praise and bless it with His love,
From lack I set it free.

I trust in God for all my good,
He is my rich supply.
My gift is blessed with love divine
That it may multiply.

I give the labor of my hand,
·The thoughts of mind and heart;
And so in all the Father's work
I have a happy part.

The hymns of Unity tell the story of what
Unity believes. Take a melody such as "Sun
of My Soul" and you will find the words to be
Unity's familiar "Prayer of Faith":

God is my help in every need;
God does my every hunger feed,
God walks beside me, guides my way
Through every moment of the day.

I now am wise, I now am true,
Patient, kind, and loving, too;
All things I am, can do, and be,
Through Christ the Truth, that is in me.

God is my health, I can't be sick;
God is my strength, unfailing, quick;

God is my all, I know no fear,
Since God and Love and Truth are here.
                    —Hannah More Kohaus

"The Doxology," known to every Christian as "Praise God from Whom All Blessings Flow," takes on a new note in Unity when it says:

Praise God that Good is everywhere;
Praise to the Love we all may share,
The Life that thrills in you and me;
Praise to the Truth that sets us free.

So, in contrast to much of the programming of the decade of the 1980s as the exasperation point of God's wrath and patience, is Unity's onward going, upbeat vision of hope and faith, keynoted on God as a loving Father. Aware of the paradox but meeting it on its own terms, is Unity's Christ-centered consciousness, ministered in the field by the AUC, enforced by Silent Unity's unwavering voice, and certified by Unity's publications.

There was a morning when, while waiting to board a plane at Los Angeles International Airport, I was jolted into remembering the lesson I had read in that day's DAILY WORD (September 21, 1981). It was titled,

"God in Charge." Its opening sentences were to the effect that: *The prophets of doom do not discourage me. I do not accept destructive views. I bless the world and God is still in charge.*

By virtue of life's uncanny timing in which we all are continually involved, a young bearded man with religious tracts in hand and armed with a leather-covered Bible gave me the brother-eye and came over to where I was sitting. He wanted to talk to me about my need for being saved the "true Christian" way. Learning that I was a local resident, he assured me that Angelenos were definitely on God's hit list, the reason being that Southern California is a sinful country, earthquake country, and impassive to the impending danger of the San Andreas fault.

I told him frankly what I have often told myself, "The San Andreas fault is not my fault. It is God's fault."

The young man stared at me visibly shaken at such audacity. But only for a moment. Then his eyes lit up. "That's just it!" he exclaimed. "It's *God's* fault!" As if to say that God had the San Andreas fault as His ace in the hole and would play it any time He wished.

As I wondered about this encounter, the

well-known Unity affirmation came to mind: *No one cometh unto me except the Father hath sent him!*

True enough! Because of this young evangelist, I realized more than ever that there is a *theological* metaphysics of the kind represented by the tract dispensers, and there is a *modern* metaphysics of the kind expressed in UNITY magazine and in DAILY WORD.

But for this airport meeting, I might not have reread "God in Charge" at my first opportunity:

The prophets of doom do not discourage me. I do not accept destructive views. I pour out my love on this wonderful world. God is still in charge, and goodness and love and peace prevail.

I can add to the beauty of the world, or I can tear it down. I can contribute to growth and progress, or I can add confusion. The choice is mine. I choose to pour out love and understanding. I do not contribute negative energy by hating and resenting things I do not agree with. I believe in the outworking of good; I contribute positive energy by praising and blessing, thereby increasing the good. I let the affirmative supplant the negative, let optimism overshadow pessimism. I have faith in the goodness of God; I have faith in a just and loving world. I know that God is in charge.

And the thought came to me that there is a power in Unity we often overlook—the power of the people, the Unity congregation, the fellowship, the group, whatever you wish to call it. The people, dedicated both to the centers and to Unity headquarters, living and demonstrating in their lives the stamina of the teachings. The worshipers, the association, the students of Truth, the readers of UNITY magazine and DAILY WORD, the people of Silent Unity. All of them together are the team. They carry the ball. They plan Unity's role in the world. And that is what religion with an inter-spiritual consciousness is all about. That is part of the analogy of the river and the lake land of faith. Ministers come and ministers go, just as leaders of all kinds come and go. Decades come and go, and so do paradoxes. But always there are "the people," as if each new generation is a reincarnation of our own higher selves and an expression of a universal Unity yet to be.

Chapter II

Faith Incorporated

Unity headquarters is subject to the elements just as every other locality. Spring is bright with new life breaking out in every twig and bough, though there can be tornadoes. The summers can get unbearably hot in Jackson County, Missouri. Autumn is usually wonderful. Parts of the winter are very cold. There are mid-winter snows and occasionally good-sized drifts.

There was a January blizzard in 1978, with swirling snow and sleet, and I was waiting it out at the Kansas City airport. It was good to be on the ground, but I decided not to pick up a car and attempt to maneuver the hazardous freeways to Unity Village where I had an appointment with Charles Rickert Fillmore. I holed up at a nearby hotel where one of the entrance doors was drifted shut and part of the heating system had conked out. I mention this because when I telephoned Charles and told him I was snowbound and would have to renegotiate an onward flight to Texas where I had a speaking date the following night, he said he would drive out for our promised meeting, which he did.

He arrived, having defied the weather and icy roads, and we sat together huddled in overcoats in the frigid hotel restaurant. Charles is a man for all seasons in more ways than one.

My acquaintance with Charles Rickert reached back through the years to pleasant memories of evenings spent with him and his sister Rosemary (Rhea) in their parental home with Rick as the always engaging host. This is where my overview of Unity was constantly deepened, expanded, and endeared. I think these rare get-togethers must have had something of the transcendentalistic lift that Ralph Waldo Emerson might have generated in his day. Discussions of Unity in diversity, the power of creative thought, speculations about life after death, communication with the dead, politics, art, the international scene, God at work in history—Rick always primed up the best of thoughts from his guests. For, while Lowell and Papa Charley had new thought thinking in common, Rick and Papa Charley saw eye-to-eye in the unlimited outreach of mind, speculated on extrasensory perception, probed the yet-to-be-revealed knowledge of God, and held to the youthfulness of faith.

If Waldo Rickert Fillmore had that vision, then Charles Rickert had it, too. Charles had seen military service following his graduation from the University of Missouri in 1943, serving as executive officer aboard a U.S. Navy minesweeper during World War II. Then he returned to the religious environment in which he had grown up, back to learn about Unity anew from the ground up, to weigh it against the background of his military experiences and a world in transition. He went from a worker in the bindery department to production control manager of the printing department, then director of public relations. Charles enrolled in the Ministerial Training program, worked in Silent Unity, and subsequently went on to become Executive Vice-President of Unity School.

His credentials, however, as they would say in the trade, were considerably higher than a mere case of nepotism. Charles was the compelling force behind an updated development program which resulted in an expanded adult education curriculum and an upgraded library.

The fundamental purpose of Unity as a teaching faith was held in steady hands by Charles Rickert's presence in the scheme of things. He had serious considerations about his role in Unity, and he familiarized himself with it fully from the field ministry to the role of Unity headquarters in these years of expansion.

Charles is an outdoor person with a love for nature. He also knows the nature of man and of the world-at-large, just as Rick did.

My presumption for this observation is that I was closely involved with GIs of Charles Fillmore's age and caliber in my work at the University of Iowa during the postwar years. I knew both the challenge and the hope of the young men who came home after the war. They returned with great expectations no less than tremendous disillusionments. The precariousness of victory was pitted against the rise of nuclear power, Hiroshima, Nagasaki. The hard reality of religion's role in war and peace was an issue for soul-searching thought. The GI bill, the future, the veterans' return to a suddenly decentralized culture and a new ideological world were, as we now realize from the vantage point of time, a prelude to the later frustration of Vietnam.

I remember accompanying a group of GIs of the Catholic faith to a Trappist monastery in Iowa in the early 1950s where they joined the rigorous Cistercian order as if in a desperate attempt to recycle their disillusioned spiritual lives. I know the tremendous interest the young people in my classes had for an insight into world religions—Buddhism, Hinduism, and the like—as if in the hope that an interfaith approach might hold some practical answer to their quest.

My reason for this recall is something that gave me a deeper insight into Charles Rickert Fillmore who was to become President of Unity School of Christianity in 1972, three years before the passing of Lowell.

In the early 1960s I escorted a delegation of eleven Japanese religious leaders across America on a month-long tour. The purpose was "A Goal for Peace Through Spiritual Understanding," and one of our most important stops was Unity Village, where the chairman and host for our group was Charles. He and his father Rick introduced our delegation to the Kansas City Rotary Club for an unforgettable meeting of what the national media called "an adventure in international understanding through religious interchange."

It must be remembered that this was little more than ten years following the signing of the Peace Treaty with Japan (1951), the de-

deification of Hirohito, the memories of Pearl Harbor, the internment of American-Japanese in detention camps, and the climax of the first nuclear holocaust. Now here were eleven Japanese clergymen representing Shinto, Buddhist, and new emerging groups in the Japanese religious scene. The combined membership of their followers was estimated at an astonishing 18,000,000. The interpreter, since none of the group spoke English, was Colbert Kurokawa, a Japanese Christian from Kyoto.

It was at the Rotary luncheon that Reverend Toshio Miyake of the Konkokyo religion thanked the Fillmores and Unity for our three-day stay at Unity Village. Through interpreter Kurokawa, Miyake, a dignified Japanese cleric, began his address to the Rotarians with a superb Japanese-ism that found its way into the American press. Said Miyake, "One seeing is better than a hundred hearings!"

It was his way of describing the reaction of the group to what they had found at Unity headquarters. Each stop along our American tour had been special: the Mormon Temple at Salt Lake, the Baha'i Temple in Wilmette, Islamic centers, Jewish synagogues, Catholic and Protestant churches and headquarters,

Unity churches in Santa Monica, Detroit, and Miami, universities from coast to coast—Unity Village was the peak experience. It represented a spiritual bond that these heads of Japan's powerful religions deeply felt: Unity in diversity and *world peace through spiritual understanding.*

Charles Rickert sponsored a special luncheon-banquet in Unity Inn's Gold Room at which Catholic, Protestant, and Jewish representatives, and faculty members from nearby Methodist and Nazarene colleges shared their enthusiasm for this kind of interfaith fellowship. I, too, felt it was the climax in my month-long travel with these dedicated delegates, all of whom I had met during my postwar research trips to the Land of the Rising Sun.

Charles Rickert, in his evaluation of Unity, said, "I believe its teachings can make one's life an adventure, because Unity arouses interest in our spiritual nature."

Unity's teachings were, for the Japanese religionists, a pattern and a plan, for they, too, believed in freedom of thought and a practical approach to faith's function in life. Their basic aims were "Unity centered" in their emphasis on spiritual healing, peace of mind, world peace, happiness, prosperity,

and the realization of the "God within." And
Rev. Miyake confided in me his deep and
abiding awareness of the Christ consciousness in his own worldwide work
centered at Osaka, Japan. These men were
never to forget Unity centers and Unity
Village.

"One seeing is better than a hundred hearings!" The graphic phrase stayed with me
long after the Japanese tour ended. I think of
it now as I return to Unity headquarters in
the 1980s and as I again visit with Charles
Rickert. Seeing him, strong, confident,
steady-handed, and capable administrator of
the parent organization of worldwide Unity, I
again see qualities of Rick in him no less than
something of the nature of Lowell, and evidences of Unity's original cofounders. His
father's determinism, Lowell's awareness,
and Charles and Myrtle's will to see the facts
rather than being lured away by "a hundred
hearings" are clearly evident in Charles'
leadership.

His home in Unity Village is next door to
The Arches. Charles and his wife Anne
brought up their two daughters, Harriet and
Constance, in the Unity tradition with its emphasis on freedom in careers and beliefs.

When Charles became President of Unity

School, and earlier in his capacity of Executive Vice-President, his concern for the movement took him on speaking and visitation trips around the Unity world circuit. He was concerned about how the headquarters and the ministry could more effectively serve each other. Unity churches, which numbered 102 in the 1940s, 220 in the 1960s, were now well over the 300 mark in the early 1980s.

The ministerial training program is based at Unity Village, the adult teaching facilities are here, and ordinations and licensings take place at the Village.

This is the national and international center for Unity retreats. I have been here when all the delegates were from Great Britain, and on another occasion there was an all-German delegation. Unity's DAILY WORD is published in a dozen foreign languages with English editions going into many foreign countries, and it may well be that someone, at sometime from each of these homelands has been at this American village where the tower stands.

Youth conferences, educators' conferences, ministerial conferences of many kinds, religious conferences of many faiths, ever and again, this is the place.

In the history of American faiths, and

world faiths for that matter, the continuity of the religion called Unity has an enviable record. Most movements are schismatic from their very start or become fragmented early on the way. One need only read the story of Catholic and Protestant movements to realize the truly divisive nature of Christianity. Only in recent years have there been signs of reconciliation in mergers and ecumenical programs.

Throughout Unity's first hundred years the relationship between the burgeoning field ministry and the "home office" had, with few exceptions, been "united in Unity." The exceptions include a Unity church in Los Angeles that decided to go the Pentecostal way, the occasional defection of a center on personal or social issues, and the desire of certain Unity ministers to build their own fountainheads or foundations.

Necessary to the overall understanding of Unity's Educational department is to recognize that there are cooperative programs in which Unity headquarters and the Unity ministry share responsibility. The Unity ministry itself would come under this classification as we have seen in the training program. There is also cooperative sharing in the spiritual vacation retreat activities and in the Unity School for Religious Studies (USRS).

USRS offers a program designed for self-realization and spiritual growth for people of all faiths. Courses which include biblical, metaphysical, philosophical, counseling, and self-discovery studies may be taken "on campus" at Unity Village or in local Unity centers wherever accredited teachers and ministers are able to arrange and fulfill the curriculum requirements. Certificates and diplomas are awarded to students upon satisfactory completion of the required credits for graduation.

That there could be other training programs in other locations in other years is a subject often talked about both at headquarters and in the field. There could conceivably be ministerial training centers in places other than Unity Village. An experimental ministerial training program has been started in Detroit, whereby initial training is taken in that city, then students take a year of training at the Village.

East coast, West coast, north or south, Unity is a city without walls. There was a time when Unity was looking for people, now people are looking for Unity and its principles and techniques. Within my span of research I have heard Unity condemned for beliefs that were considered heretical, and I have lived to hear them endorsed as a "new orthodoxy." Unity of today is praised for its contribution to the religious spirit of modern time. Unity of tomorrow will be challenged to present plans and programming for the Christic age now in the making. All of which is what happens when a new state of consciousness is let loose in the world.

No matter what the proliferation of Unity in the days to come or when or how the expansion of the work is instrumented through progressive vision, Unity School of Christianity is the polestar guiding the movement into the coming century.

There is in astronomy a process called the binary system. It represents two stars revolving around each other under the influence of their mutual gravitational attraction. To the naked eye the stars appear to be one, but to telescopic sight they are shown to be separate, revolving around a common center in the cosmos.

In thinking of the Association of Unity Churches and of Unity headquarters, what seems to be one is actually a binary system operating, because of a mutual affinity, around the center of a spiritual attraction.

They are two but they are one. And so deep-seated is the set of the stars, so great is the firmament in which they move, that all light emanating from Unity School is one with the light from Unity centers.

The visualization took on added meaning as I talked with Executive Vice-President Constance Fillmore in her office in the administration building. I met her for the first time when visiting one day in the 1950s, with her parents, Charles and Anne. She was quite young then. She was still young now, but with a maturity of mind that was already indicated when she was chosen valedictorian of her high school graduating class. Her advanced education began at Wellesley, was marked by a Bachelor's degree in psychology and graduation with honors from Pomona, and continued into Unity's Ministerial School and ordination in 1976.

I cannot help but speculate that there is a great deal of the Myrtle Fillmore mind and quality in Connie. Wellesley and Pomona are colleges of high academic standards and fully as eclectic as was Oberlin in Myrtle Page's day.

As I discussed with Connie how she came into Unity, not by right of birth alone but philosophically and spiritually, I realized that it was a decision of heart and mind spun on a vision of Unity's potential in meeting the challenges of our incalculable times. Somewhere in Unity, she feels, any situation can be met by the Unity teachings, and not only met but made divine.

What impresses me is Connie's vision of Unity as creating an atmosphere for the new way of life to happen. It may require what she called "a leap in consciousness," but in it is a foreshadowing of the coming of a new individual for the new age.

Surely I am not the only one who recognizes that Connie finds herself where her great-grandmother Myrtle, the mother of Unity, once played an equally dynamic role.

The similarities do not end there. Connie is a writer in her own right as Myrtle was. During her five years as a copy editor in the Editorial department of Unity School, she frequently contributed articles to UNITY magazine, produced teaching material for Unity Sunday schools, and assisted in the editing of books and manuscripts. I remember one of her UNITY magazine articles particularly, "The Courage of Their Convictions," in which she shared the dreams of students who dared follow their inner guidance and related this determination to Charles

Fillmore and ... *the Truth ideas and miracle healings that [he and] Myrtle had witnessed ... He sincerely believed that there existed a new, better way of life and he set out to live it.*

... Many of the concerns of youth today, she said, *lead them right back to a consideration of God: the growing awareness of environmental problems; the return to an appreciation of natural things; an increased interest in Eastern thought and meditation; a growing feeling of the equality of all people, regardless of sex or religion or color. There is an openness to new ideas and a freedom of thought among young people that is refreshing to see, and if they flounder occasionally in their attempts to express themselves, surely that does not lessen the import of what they are trying to accomplish.*

Connie's words do not need the support of Myrtle's convictions, but it is significant that the mother of Unity once said: *The opinions of others cannot get you down or lift you up. You have the power of God within you to raise yourself up to where you know you are His child with ability along all lines and with freedom to do whatever you really wish to do.*

Discussing with Connie and others at Unity Village their views on holism, I would foresee that Unity's program in the years ahead will attain more and more leadership in the holistic field. The spiritual direction of religion during the upcoming decades is toward a church responsible for the health and well-being of the total person. "Mind is all, and all is Mind," carries a more inclusive meaning than it did in early New Thought days. We are finally becoming aware of the powerful significance of a Christian commitment on a holistic scale. So much so that workshops in holism are suggesting that if the body *is* the temple of God, physical exercise should be part of that temple's ritual.

If the human mind manifests both conscious and subconscious phases of expression, then by all means: *Let this mind be in you [us] which was also in Christ Jesus.* (Phil. 2:5 A.V.)

Spiritual consciousness is leading the way, and eventually the societal or "race consciousness" will follow. But there is also an interesting phenomenon at work in which we may rightly catch a glimpse of divine order. I mean that, as we recognize the *human* potential, we develop *spiritual* awareness just as spiritual potential influences physical awareness. It works both ways. My own interest in various organizations stressing Christian principles in the athletic field convinces me that improved health inspires a nearness to God, and a nearness to God reflects itself in improved health. The Christ in me salutes the Christ in you, Unity says. And this Christ is a total, universal Christ.

The state of things, in terms of religious organizations generally, has all too long been an objectification of the range of one's possibilities without sufficient internalization of these possibilities.

An understanding of this suggests a deeper commitment to basic Truth principles and the experiential application of these principles in the context of life-styles and life's challenges.

I had a feeling, following my meetings with members of the Unity administrative and departmental staffs, that two biblical proverbs rather well suggest the basic thrust—and challenge—of Unity's tomorrow. Both are Solomonic injunctions:

Remove not the ancient landmark, which thy fathers have set. (Prov. 22:28)

But the path of the just is as the shining light, that shineth more and more into the perfect day. (Prov. 4:18 A.V.)

The juxtaposition or, rather, the proper balance of these dramatic axioms clearly states the issue, not of Unity only, but of all religions moving into the apocalyptic future.

Unity, however, is in a most favorable position. Its ancient landmarks are definitely Christ-centered. Its 100-year-old history has proved principles of modern metaphysics, transcendentalism, and New Thought thinking. Its ancient landmark of how life can be lived totally was already holistic with Charles and Myrtle Fillmore.

In the very beginning of Unity, when, like the time of creation, it was seemingly without form—and void—Myrtle Fillmore said in one of her "Healing Letters" something so contemporary of our time that every holistic center should have the words tacked up on a wall, or better, etched in mind:

We must agree to think health, and to bless the body and to express that which causes all the functions of the organism to work perfectly. But there is the physical side of health also. Spirit must have substance through which to manifest. You must provide the manifest substance and life elements in proper food and drink, and sunshine and air. Without these, Spirit would have no vehicle. We must know the chemistry of the body. We must find the whole man.

Or, as we are saying today, the total person—the holistic person. And, as Charles Fillmore pointed out in *Keep a True Lent, Every follower of Jesus . . . follows the way of prayer and fasting that He taught His disciples. He revealed that prayer and fasting are the sure way to spiritual power, the way to keep the soul cleansed and purified that it may feel the presence of God . . . Prayer and fasting . . . are matters of communion with God, not matters of public display.*

Touch modern holism at any of its truly vital points and you touch Unity.

In a holistic seminar at which I mentioned the Platonistic saying that, "Health is a matter of a love affair between the organs of the body," someone said, "That's Unity!"

So, in fact, is Plato's metaphor that every individual represents a team of horses and the driver. The horse called Body wishes to remain earth-centered; the horse called Mind, like Pegasus, wishes to soar and try its wings. Spirit is the Driver who holds the reins.

That holistic living was an ancient landmark in the Unity movement is clearly demonstrated in the lives of the Fillmore founding family. And the more the Fillmore writings are examined the more abundant become references to total living as a basic principle in the early years of the movement.

In 1928 Myrtle Fillmore wrote to a prominent nutritionist, Dr. Bengamin Hauser, for suggestions on multidimensional living. *There will come a time,* she said in her letter, *when we can draw forth the universal mind stuff, just the elements we need in the right proportion and relation, to maintain the proper balance in our organisms. We shall be able to draw chemical substances from the fourth dimensional realm, down into our physical body. But in the meantime, we need to make practical all the knowledge we have concerning bodily renewal, through using intelligence and discrimination in the selection of our food . . . I am asking your help, and shall be glad for anything that you can tell me, to help along the work of bodily transformation and renewal.*

Meantime Charles Fillmore was speaking about, and writing about, and attempting to live in accordance with what he called *Dynamics for Living. Lack of health is not prevalent in God's universe,* he asserted. *If such lack appears anywhere it is the work of man!*

As Myrtle evidenced her interest by contacting Dr. Hauser, so Charles Fillmore got in touch with life extensionist Paul Bragg, with whom I had close association during the 1970s. Paul told me that in the "olden days," that is, the early days of Unity, he assisted Papa Charley in formulating nutritional menus for the cafeteria at the Tracy headquarters. Charles Rickert Fillmore verified this interesting historic note by sharing with me a portion of the correspondence that passed between his grandfather Charles and Dr. Bragg. Currently, books by Bragg are being reprinted because of their value in the contemporary holistic movement, and I would predict that Charles Fillmore's publications will hold an increasing interest and a growing readership as the holistic concept becomes important in the public mind.

Actually, we are eyewitnesses to a quiet renaissance of natural healing methods, self-responsibility, and the discovery of the "Physician within."

From Unity's inception, its recognition of the holistic impact of the Man of Galilee was one of its "ancient landmarks." It emphasized that He was the prototype of the new person for a new age. He was the example in the integration of body, mind, and Spirit, demonstrating the amplitude of this in "miracle healings," urging His followers to recognize the wholeness and holiness within themselves. He asked them to look upon the body as the temple of God, the mind as the divine channel of expression of God's will, and the Spirit as the innate life of God manifested in every person and everything in nature's world.

Since this is a landmark of the Unity movement, headquarters and the ministry recognize its value and will see that it is not removed but that it is projected in a continuing *shining light* (Prov. 4:18) as the Solomonic proverb suggests. This would be done by way of vital, innovative, and demonstrable principles old in Truth and modern in spirit. The perspective of that light must surely include holism in its many forms, and particularly, for Unity, a developing emphasis on three indivisible disciples—the art of healing, the way of spiritual unfoldment, and the power of mind.

This will require the highest possible meaning of the binary process mentioned earlier, the mutual gravitational pull playing upon both Unity headquarters and the ministry in the field. Toward this, it would appear, both the present administration at Unity Village and the planning of the Association of Unity Churches are being geared.

The view of researchers in religions of the

world has always been that a "minimum view" of Jesus, His life, His miracles, His impact, was that He spoke with authority because He lived what He believed. He was a challenging figure. He was moved by love and compassion. He may or may not have had the building of a church or a denomination in mind. With unquestioning faith He restored faith, self-confidence, hope, and credibility to sick and lost souls. He lifted the fallen and compelled the mighty to take a deeper look at Truth.

For myself, the adventure in Unity is one that comes down—or up—to every seeking soul. Within its shallows and its depths one thought is always just beneath the surface, "God and I—God and you." Which is, no doubt, why "the Christ in me salutes the Christ in you"—in Unity.

Chapter III

Of Time and the Tower

In 1962 when the first edition of "The Unity Way of Life" appeared under the Prentice-Hall imprint, gasoline was twenty-five cents a gallon, gold was thirty-five dollars an ounce, the prime rate five-and-a-quarter percent. A room in a quality motel could be had for six dollars, coffee was five cents a cup, movies were fifty cents, with popcorn (buttered) at a nickel a bag.

I was thinking of this now, twenty years later, as I began the 200-step climb to the top of Unity's tower, determined to see if the view of the countryside had changed as radically as the commerce of our changing times.

It is not the *cost* of living that tantalized me on this particular May morning, it was the *value* of living as we find it in society-at-large and in ourselves as individuals. I was thinking of Unity today, its concepts and teachings, how it has outlived most of its critics and converted others, not in an evangelistic sense, but in the sheer adventurousness and practicality of principles to live by in our contemporary, swiftly changing world. And I was thinking of my first "investigation" of Unity nearly a half century ago.

"Nearly a half century" stops me in my tracks. Time is a magician. Time is the innovator, the leveler, "the clocksetter." Time, the arbiter of Truth.

I am forced to confess that my years in the exciting wilderness of religious research around the world actually began with an appraisal of Unity in my first book on America's emerging religions: "They Have Found a Faith" (Bobbs-Merrill, 1946). It was a breakthrough book, reviewers said, in that it took an "empathic look" at movements which in those days were commonly discounted and ridiculed as cults, sects, and spin-off groups from the established faiths. I said in this first of many books on the emerging religions of the world: *Let others turn ecclesiastical microscopes on these new faiths or weigh them on their scales of* final truth, *I will devote myself more to the* way *than to the* why *of their doctrines. I will content myself with the age-old verdict of Gamaliel, "If this work be of men, it will come to nought, but if it be of God, it will endure."*

I remembered Unity's climb to recognition

as I climbed the stairs. I could have taken the elevator to the seventh floor, which is as far as it ordinarily goes, but I wanted to walk, not to test my stamina but to follow a certain guidance and to stand once more atop the tower, where I stood with Waldo Rickert Fillmore in Unity's wilderness years, when it was seeking its destined place in the world's expanding spiritual scene. Each step in the spiraling stairway is prologue to the past and the prospect of a new, upcoming century of Unity progress.

Here I was, with permission to use this seemingly abandoned stairway passage for the sake of sentiment and recall. Not that the tower building is abandoned; far from it. It is, as always, teeming with activity.

The world of Unity, I told myself, has always had three worlds in mind: an inner world, an outer world, and an overworld. It is the first of these, the inner world, that had me in its spell just now. The darksome, silent surroundings of this monolithic structure have a haunting way of bringing back the Fillmore metaphor that the spiritual climb of life is spiral. The personal quest is an inner world ascent in consciousness. It is a staircase, spiraled.

My impression of the Fillmore family of

faith, Charles and Myrtle, Lowell, Rick, and Royal, had always been that they were not exceptional people following an ordinary pattern, but ordinary people dedicated to a pattern exceptionally extraordinary. They were human beings, driven not by a desire for deification but by a passion for Truth that meets human needs through a mental equivalent higher than human mind.

Surely, as far as the inner world is concerned, they would have felt, as I was feeling now, that the elevator of total living, even as the tower elevator, goes only so far. At some point we are challenged to climb. Sometimes the space is cramped, as I found it to be on this stairway, literally and figuratively, cramped between body and mind. Higher up there is always room to spare. The higher one climbs, the less crowded the path. Often along the way the air is stuffy and there is need for ventilation, particularly in one's thinking. The handrail is slippery. You often wish you had more of a handle on things to support your climbing. The way is often unclear, like a tunnel set on end, upside down.

I could almost see Rick smiling in his amused way at one's tendency to solve things merely by the use of the rational mind, when there is so much of wonder in the world that must be caught intuitively.

Unity, in its rendezvous with the inner world, the world of consciousness, will in the days ahead ask its people to remember more and more that they carry a light. They are light bearers by way of the Christ within, whose light casts no frightening shadow, only reassuring good. The tower is an architectural symbol of our inner world encounter. The spiral ascent continues throughout life. The light we carry is eternal. Handrail or no handrail, space or the lack of it, the darker the way the more penetrating the light.

How clear life's episodes seem when viewed in retrospect or when we view them from above! It is the uncharted that presents the challenge and asks us to decide whether the climb is to be an adventure or an aggravation.

The inner world of Unity is the adventure personally lived, quietly experienced as a partnership with God.

Admittedly, I was thinking idealistically, but that is because so many Unity leaders and people have shared their stories with me, and because I have found their beliefs and theories workable in my own experiences.

There was, for example, the Unity minister who told me about her dog. She had this dog, a wirehaired terrier with all the erratic temperament of its breed. I had a wirehaired, too. He was lovable but uncontrollable. Hers was loving without having lost his alertness and his spark.

I asked her how she had trained her dog. She assured me he had once been as ambivalent as mine, but her discipline was simple. She began to visualize him as "God's little dog." Holding him in that consciousness, that is what he became.

I began using the same technique on my Nickie, suspecting that I had already erred by giving him a name reminiscent of "Old Nick." No matter. My wife and I began reminding him and treating him and assuring him that he was "God's little dog."

One bright day in early spring while working in my study on the second floor of our home, I happened to look out of the window and see flecks of white floating like snowflakes in the lightly stirring breeze. Upon closer observation, the mystery was immediately clear. My wife had put several pillows out for airing and Nickie was on a rampage. He had ripped one open and was shaking the feathers out of it in terrier delight. I shouted at him. I shouted to my wife, "Better check on God's little dog!" She went out and I went down and we had a family conference that ended with Nickie locked in the kitchen.

I went back to my desk. An hour or so later, my wife came up to the study. Gently she took my hand. Quietly she led me to the window. Silently we stood looking down. There on the lawn in the warmth of spring were several birds, linnets, picking up the feathers for the building of their nests. God's little dog had fulfilled a mission.

This inner world awareness is part of the Unity game of life—and thought. It all seems romantically simple when one can count the steps and know precisely how far it is to the top, to the greater light of understanding.

In my case, here in the tower, light was beginning to show itself, beckoning from an open door above my head. I realized, as I looked up, that the door had already been opened for my convenience, as if to say that there are always anonymous forces at work in one's inner world.

Several more steps and I was at the fresh and open portals of this campanile. I stood on the observation platform in the cupola. Here, as I adjusted to the sunlight and felt the gentle wind, the inner world was still, but the outer world was, for the moment, completely overwhelming me.

Talk about the change in the cost of living and the commerce of the world—take a look at this! I mean, no matter which way you turned, the view on all sides confirmed beyond the shadow of doubt that the once geographic setting of open meadows and sprawling space had been totally swallowed up, absolutely devoured by relentless change. There is the Western Electric plant. Nearby the Pfizer Chemical Company. Crowding upon them is John Knox Village, a city for senior citizens built by ambitious developers to fill a need, but adding nonetheless to a megalopolis whose suburban areas expire in a maze of freeways and traffic as far as eye can see. The entire circumference of this once rural woodland is building, still in labor, so to say. It is challenging the mapmakers and the demographers to keep pace with the meta-morphosis poised for the decades ahead.

The only seemingly changeless site is Unity Village. It remains, as always, bounded on the south by orchards, on the east by a lake and woods, then circled by trees and hedges that hide the lanes of traffic and soften the sound of cars almost to a pleasantness. I was again looking at a bit of England judging by the Cotswold country style homes, a touch of

Spain or Portugal when viewing the colored tiles, a scene out of Italy with the bridge across a channel of fountains, cloistered walks and colonnades, or a place in anywhere where architecture fits into nature's scheme. But, though the scene was international, it was still a living segment of Americana in the tradition of our heritage of faith.

I realized again that the outer world as far as Unity is concerned is not a threat but an opportunity, a fact that has been evidenced many times in my own Unity experiences. There was a happening in the New York center that I often remember when challenges for a "miracle" confront me. I was giving a series of lectures on spiritual healing when an elderly woman asked whether we might have special prayer with her. For a year and a half she had been unable to walk without the use of a cane. The condition of lameness had begun when she and a friend were crossing a street and a careening car struck and killed her companion. The woman agreed that, since she herself was not hit, her inability to walk could be a matter of traumatism, a negative transference, a psychomotor disturbance, or whatever. She had gone the rounds of psychoanalysts and medical consultants and was still wedded to her cane and an uneasiness about herself as real as if it were pathological. The outer world had preempted her inner world of faith.

We spent half an hour together in prayer and spiritual attunement. We spoke our affirmations of healing aloud. We meditated silently. We held hands in a consciousness of God's special presence in this consultation room. I remember the quiet confidence with which I went to the opposite side of the room and asked her to walk over to me. I remember her expression when she said, "Without my cane?" Her incredulity was already tempered by a hint of sudden faith.

I said to her, "God is your cane."

In that moment my faith was unshakable. So was hers. She took a step ever so haltingly. Then another as she balanced herself uncertainly, and a third which led into a series of steps and a reach for my outstretched hands. We repeated this wall-to-wall walking while she wept and thanked God and cheered up and thanked Him some more.

When I walked with her through the reception room, carrying her cane, the hostess said, "What happened?" We made it clear that she was walking with God.

I went with her down the outside stairs and gave her the cane. She put it behind her back, locked an arm around each end of it, confident that no obstacle could ever again stand in her way.

But the point of the story came back to me with new meaning when I put it into the context of the inner world and the outer world as I was seeing it from the tower. For the truth is that when I left the woman at the bottom of the steps on 55th and Broadway she was still standing there when I went down for lunch half an hour later. She stood huddled in a corner leaning on her cane. When I said to her, "What's the matter?" she looked at me as if for the first time. "I can't do it," she said. "I can't cross the street. Look at the traffic. I can't!"

I took her hand and said, "God is your cane!"

She suddenly stood tall. Whatever she was seeing was no greater than her faith. Whatever she had heard was all she needed.

"God is my cane!" she whispered to herself and put the cane behind her back, through the crook of her arms, and off she marched.

The next Sunday she came to the service at Carnegie Hall, walking with God.

Unity, I told myself, *is not designed to hold back the outer world of traffic and growth and challenges, but to provide viable spiritual power to meet the world's impulsive forward thrust.*

How does it accomplish this? With a vision of the overworld, a world already existing in universal Mind and in human consciousness, which now needs to be made collective in a unity of Spirit.

Surely it was this overworld Charles Fillmore had in mind when he said: *Our attention in this day is being largely called to the revolution that is taking place in the economic world, but a revolution of even greater worth is taking place in the mental and spiritual worlds. A large and growing school of metaphysicians has made its advent in this generation, and it is radically changing the public mind toward religion. In other words, we are developing spiritual understanding, and this means that religion and its sources in tradition and in man are being inquired into and its principles applied in the development of a new cosmic mind for the whole human family. So we need a larger realization of the importance of man and the importance of every one of us in manifesting the God who is Spirit.*

As the gist of these words came to me, the inner world and the outer world were synthesized in an overworld as surely as the meadowland where Unity Village now stands was transformed into a living center of faith and prayer. Here, it seemed to me, was the grand denouement.

Consider that Fillmore's words were spoken nearly half a century ago and published in 1949 in a book with the astonishing title, *Atom-Smashing Power of Mind.* Perhaps the title was too sensational to have caught public attention in a day when sensationalism was constantly interpreted on the basis of orthodoxy. Perhaps the book should have been called "The Phenomenon of Man."

No, that title was reserved by divine order for another revolutionary thinker let loose on planet Earth, Teilhard de Chardin, the Roman Catholic, the paleontologist, the heretic who may one day become a saint in the church that banished him for his heterodoxical views.

Teilhard, as every Unity minister knows, was speaking in scientific terms, in theological terms, in evolutionary terms of the identical theme that Charles Fillmore had presented in the sweep and spirit of inspired metaphysics. The theme was "cosmogenesis": the convergence of the mind of man and the Mind of God. Someday someone will do a comparative scholarly study of these two books and these two men and show how Fillmore saw unity as being the nature of things, and how Teilhard viewed the nature of things as being in unity. Each emphasized with convincing power the "Christic" energy in the overworld of which we speak.

These are the depths with which Unity is challenged to deal in its tomorrow. The magnitude of Fillmore's "interthinking" is still to be discovered. It is in his *Atom-Smashing Power of Mind* and in his *Twelve Powers of Man* that the true metaphysical stature of the cofounder of Unity reveals itself. It is in his *Keep a True Lent* that his views of psychosocial relationship are manifested. He must be read with an inner eye of understanding to truly grasp the implications of Unity's place in the spiritual unfoldment of the years ahead.

It is in these books that Fillmore also reveals his inseparable kinship with Emerson. It is here that the father of Unity and the father of New Thought would both receive the blessings of Teilhard de Chardin. For Fillmore and Emerson in probing the phenomenon of man discover the phenomenon of God. It is here that "man" becomes all humanity and God assumes the amplitude of Universal Mind. It is here that modern metaphysics is challenged to keep step with science and with the unlimited activity of human thought.

Time and the tower were plainly speaking and, for the moment, speaking plainly. They were saying that it would be necessary for Unity to look at itself as a legacy to be passed on through its youth and its total constituency. And this, in fact, is where the thrust of Unity is directed. A hundred years of history have implanted it firmly in people on the quest and challenged them to grasp its merit in the spiral climb of faith.

Fillmore would show more interest than astonishment at the realization that all religions have come around to his insistence that thoughts create physical and psychological conditions in individuals and society as well. To be sure, he was not the originator of the theory, but he was its fearless advocate. He would be pleased to find that science has proved that thought creates chemical and electromagnetic effects on bodily organs, that the set of mind triggers biochemical changes, affects the mitotic division of cells, causes health or disease according to the mental indwelling on constructive or destructive modes of thinking. He would be grateful to know that his "twelve powers of man" theory has received the endorsement of metaphysicians. And he could not help but pause in wonder to realize that his once controversial view of contemplating biological years in terms of a life span rather than on a statistical life expectancy is part of today's avowed holistic emphasis.

I am not a qualified futurist, but as I look from the tower and see the Unity Village teaching facilities, from its retreat to its adult training programs, with its breadth of spiritual outreach from Silent Unity to the busy Activities Center, I realize that here is a base of learning for all people, a "town without walls." In a modern mystical sense, it is the overworld embodying the instars and the imago of the overchurch.

It includes the physicist whose thoughts have penetrated outer space, the historian whose study has followed the footprints of God through the rise and fall of civilizations, the scientist who has unlocked the secret doors of the inner mind, the philosopher who has spied a harmony in the once inharmonious schools of thought, the educator who perceives a divine power beyond no less than within the intellectual process, the industrialist who has caught on to a workable ethic in his business dealings, the theologian who recognizes a divine power as the common ground of all being; in short it embraces men and women of every walk of life who realize that religion is an adventure in search and discovery—all these constitute a dispersed spiritual potential, the new church, which has yet to be made collective.

For Unity knows, as I know, that above and beyond the things that separate various religions are Truths which unite them, and that while many groups are divided by nonessentials, the great essentials are being discovered, often outside the bounds of the institutionalized, traditional denominations.

Ask sincere, thinking people what they are looking for in the way of a vital, contemporary religion, and they will tell you something like this: I think religion should keep a person healthy in body, active in mind, and joyful in spirit. It should assist one in maintaining that fine balance between loving the world and denying the world, of enjoying the world without losing the spiritual perspective, of being successful in the world without making success the final goal. Give me a faith that makes demands of me and one of which I can make demands, a faith that has the Christ in it—not a vague, theological Christ, but One who gives me a sense of identification. Give me techniques and affirmations, and words to live by, and, most of all, give me examples of the workability of faith in living people so that I may better see what I, too, may become.

Unity as an eclectic faith fills this prescription. Like America, it is an amalgam, and therein lies its genius and its strength. As America has absorbed the cultures of the world and has benefited by the best motives of the world's people, so Unity has profited by the thought and discoveries of the world's religions. I would guess that it has received much because it has given much; and this, of course, is basic as a Unity principle.

The God of Unity is so great that He can never express Himself fully in one denomination or compress Himself into one exclusive sect. He is a prism through which the one light is refracted. He is the sea from which and into which the rivers of thought are flowing. He is love eternal, out of which love in its myriad forms expresses itself. He is God, and being God, He is the one Presence, the one Power.

I am reminded again that you can be a good member of Unity and still worship in other faiths, for the object of worship is always God as Principle, God as Love, and God as Truth. You can sit yoga fashion, if you wish, or enter the satori of Zen and say your prayers, and be a Unity follower. You can walk the eightfold path of the Buddha without straying from Unity teaching and beliefs. You can bow five times toward Mecca and still be Unity conscious. You can stand before the tomb of your ancestors, as does the Confucianist and the Taoist: you can say a prayer of gratitude for the influence and heritage of a departed loved one without denying what Unity believes. You can sit before the sacred fire of the Parsees and gaze into the holy flames, if the Parsi priest will let you, without losing your Unity point of view. You can stand with the Jew over the holy Torah, or walk with the Shintoist through his sacred groves, or chant an affirmation with the Hindu on the banks of the Ganges—you can do all these things and still be a student of Unity because there is within you a living flame of understanding that warms you with the knowledge that the spirit of God is one Spirit, and that He is sovereign over all creeds.

As the Christ becomes greater to you in Unity, the founders and teachers of other faiths also become greater; and the greater they become, the greater the Christ becomes. That is true of your estimate of all prophets when you know the prophet Jesus Christ. He who lives in all lives in you, and because He lives, all people live more gloriously, more richly, and with more subtle insight than they lived before. There are those who will not understand this paradox, but Unity understands it and lives by it as an expression of Truth.

They know that people cannot be argued into religion, they must be loved into it. And that is the challenge that the future holds.

Chapter IV

The Unity Way

When you sum it all up, life is largely a matter of coming and going, packing and unpacking, saying hello and good-bye with worlds of wonder in between.

A nice thing about Unity is that leave-taking is softened by saying, "There is no parting in Spirit," which is another clue to the way in which it seeks to make all phases of life an adventure in faith.

Here I am packing my bags, sorting through a briefcase, getting a scramble of notes in order, and contemplating whether to do some typing before closing up the portable.

It is 8:30 a.m. I have jogged around the golf course and the orchard on this mid-May morning, and I have also been fortified with an excellent cafeteria breakfast and a quiet reading of DAILY WORD. I am flying home to California this afternoon.

For the past week my residence here has been the Unity Hotel, one of the oldest, most venerable dwellings in Unity Village. Beautifully situated, this Normandy, two-and-a-half story haven has an open view of nature's unspoiled wonderland with a distant glimpse of the swimming pool, the orchard, and the well-tended, never-too-busy golf course. This is a mini-world unto itself, silent, peaceful, and cozy.

I have been quartered in the VIP room with the full privilege of the adjoining parlor, its grand piano, fireplace, and soft divans. This was my second stay in Unity Hotel, the first having been about two years ago.

VIPs who have stayed here through the years were considerably more "VIPish" than I, but I realize that, as they made the hotel famous, the hotel has made them "famouser" than they were before they came. They were touched by Unity.

Among the list of coming and going notables are such intriguing names as Edwin Markham who drew the circle of love, you recall, with the wit to win; Alan Watts, the religious vagabond who wrote and felt deeply about the spiritual oneness of all faiths; Victor Frankl, psychiatrist-existentialist; Pir Vilayat Inayat Khan, Sufi mystic; Emmet Fox, author and renowned minister of the Church of the Healing Christ; Norman Vincent Peale, author of "The Power of Positive

Thinking"; Lieutenant Colonel James B. Irwin, astronaut of Apollo XV; Charles King, beloved singer-song leader and friend of Unity; Wally Amos of "Famous Amos" cookie fame; actors and actresses: Ann Francis, Spring Byington, Jayne Meadows, Steve Allen, John Payne; and poetess Bonita Granville.

No matter how great the celebrities, there was one thing I held in common with them, or they with me: We all came and went. And in the coming and going there is a universal tie with everyone, and all of us are VIPs to someone, somewhere, at some time along the way.

It is doubtful, however, whether anyone has had more serendipitous happenings in Unity sojourns than I. The people I have run into by chance, the fateful crisscrossing of lines, the unexpected meetings with people all around the world tied-in, in some way, with Unity. I am thinking during these moments of one departure from Unity Village recounted years ago in *The Unity Way of Life*.

I had driven here from Chicago on that occasion, and after a week's stay I was getting ready to drive back through the Saturday traffic to my post at the university. I had eaten breakfast at the cafeteria, just as I did today, and had returned to my motel room with the avowed purpose of doing some much needed last-minute writing. I had not reached VIP status in those days, but I did have Room One in the motel units.

My typewriter was set up, the yellow sheets were handily in place, and I was just settling down to type out some last-minute notes when there was a rap at the door.

My first reaction was to become annoyed, but under the circumstances of being at Unity headquarters what could I do but say to myself, "No one cometh unto me except the Father hath sent him!"

The visitor at the door was an acquaintance of long-standing who considered it a pleasant surprise to have found me. His name was Gary, a relaxed, portly, middle-aged man, a public relations counselor for a nationally known industry. He had been in New Orleans with his wife Emily where they had met her older sister Bertha, a Unity member. She was riding to Chicago with them, and since none of them had ever been to Unity Village, they decided to come by and look things over. Paging through the guest register and "by chance" spying my name, Gary decided to begin the Village tour with a stop at my motel unit.

It began to dawn on me even then that perhaps the Father *had* indeed sent him, and not only him, but his wife and her sister as well, for a more interesting and diversified trio would have been hard to find. Gary had met me at interfaith conferences in Green Lake, Wisconsin and Chicago. He was, to quote his phrase, "On a quest, just like you." So you might say he was a "seeker."

His wife Emily, outward-going, pleasantly irrepressible, flashing diamonds, and casually wearing a mink stole, knew emphatically what she believed and why she believed it. We had met previously and she was delighted that I remembered she was an Episcopalian, "Not by birth, but by choice and intellectual persuasion." You might call her an "observer."

Her sister Bertha, the Unity member, a widow, gray-haired, pleasant, with a spontaneous smile, had already been breathing deeply of the bracing Unity Village air. There was no question that she had found a faith and that Unity was it. You could call her a "convert."

Their coming, of course, put an end to my good intentions for a writing spree; but when Gary suggested that perhaps they were disrupting my day, I caught myself saying, "Not at all. I am sure that everything is in divine order," which shows how far I had come along the Unity way. In fact, I found myself assuring them I would escort them over the grounds until an official tour under a qualified guide could be arranged.

Most of all, when I began to analyze the situation, I realized it *was* all in divine order. In this trio the world had indeed come to Unity Village in the form of a seeker, an observer, and a convert. And I? Well, I was the momentary perceiver of my own adventurous quest.

Because the convert Bertha wanted to walk the grounds alone with her own thoughts and get the "feeling" of Unity Village, the seeker Gary, the observer Emily, and I strolled over to the amphitheatre for some moments in the hushed surroundings.

"How do you account for it?" the observer Emily asked with concern.

"Account for what?" her husband the seeker wanted to know.

"All of this," said Emily with a flourish that took in the hundreds of Unity acres. "I had no idea when Bertha talked about Unity that it was so pretentious. How do you account for it?"

"Why," said Gary, "you account for it on the basis that people want it and need it."

"Oh, but darling," she exhorted, "there are goodness knows how many religions in the world."

"There are goodness knows how may cars in the world, too," Gary countered, biting off the end of a cigar.

"But why another religion? Why Unity?"

Seeker Gary thought it preposterous that a religion had to account for itself any more than a new automobile had to justify its appearance. If someone had an idea for a better religion or a better car, why not put it on the market? Let the people decide.

I suggested that Unity came to create a fellowship where people are held together by the adventure of the quest and the thrill of spiritual discoveries.

"But don't all religions believe that?" asked the observer.

"If they do," I said, "that's what accounts for them. It is also what eventually makes them accountable."

"By the way," Gary spoke up with cigar lighter poised, "it's all right to smoke here, isn't it?"

I assured him it was.

"Of course some Unity members smoke," his wife declared, "and some drink, too. I'm positive they do. Don't they?"

I got myself off the hook by saying, "Moral codes vary among Unity members as they do in other liberal religions."

The discussion took us into Charles and Myrtle Fillmore's beliefs about vegetarianism, spiritual healing, and reincarnation.

"There you are!" Emily interrupted. "That's the way these new religions get started. They stress some particular phase, something sensational, and that attracts people. Now take Bertha, for example. When her husband died, she said that Unity sustained her as no other religion could possibly have done. How does she know? How could she say that? My religion sustained me when our son was killed in Japan."

"We are all different, Emily," said her husband consolingly. "One finds his answers here, another there. But a religion like Unity has a wide range of speculation. Bertha goes for that. I sort of go for that—as you do," singling me out with the glowing tip of his cigar. "I think there is more to life and death than most churches realize; more to religion generally, for that matter. A religion like Unity explains all these roads."

"What roads?" Emily challenged.

"Oh, like reincarnation. The way God works. The way prayer works. The way the power of the mind works. You see, Unity has all these sayings and things and that's good. It opens up a whole new field of experimentation."

"Experimentation in religion?" Emily exclaimed in make-believe shock. "You think that's good?"

"Well, darling," said the seeker, "the only difference is that in our church we've believed in experimentation so long we now call it doctrine and let it go at that."

"I believe it is good," I had to say, "to take this deeply personal relationship with something higher than oneself into account. A Unity follower is the kind who gets up in the morning to greet the day as if it were a new personal gift from God, and who by no means considers it odd or unrealistic to be continually thankful for the sheer fact of living."

"Well, that's Bertha all right!" the observer agreed.

"And I don't see anything wrong with it," said the seeker.

"Who said there is anything wrong with it?" replied Emily. "All I am saying is that all religions have these same things."

How far could I go without appearing to be a spokesman for Unity? I decided to let Bertha tell them sometime, if she wished, how far the Unity spirit had taken her. For my part, I secretly believed that one quality that kept Unity young and Unity believers enthusiastic was the adventurous spirit. This kept them spiritually on their toes and lured them on. For many of them, life was the drama, the playwright was God, and they were coauthors with Him in the unfoldment of the scenario.

I had to testify to both seeker and observer that since I was persuaded that *God is good*, I found Unity's principles logical and of immense practical *help*. They *helped* me turn things around and to think in terms of hypothetical cases in which divine order continually plays a role and gives one a chance for a choice, so to say.

Unity continually urged me to choose the better of the two: the higher rather than the lower impulse, the hopeful rather than the hopeless decision, the greater rather than the smaller point of view, the lovelier rather than the loveless, a God of light rather than a God of darkness.

Persuaded that every circumstance is a challenge for growth and we have a choice, life takes on a quality that adds up to an adventure. Truth is, I must have gone on quite grandiloquently about my interest in all this because the observer Emily suddenly broke in with a disarming laugh and said, "Don't you find anything in Unity to *criticize*?"

"Of course he doesn't," said Gary. "Unity has taught him to see only the good. And that's *good*!"

"I always find things to criticize," I confessed, "even in my own religion."

"Which reminds me," Emily cut in shaking an accusing finger at me, "just what *is* your religion?"

"Denominationally?" I asked.

"Denominationally."

"It is slightly involved," I conceded, "so let's simply say that I still belong to the church of my birth."

"Which is?"

"The German Reformed," I explained, "which merged with the Evangelical Synod of North America, which later merged with the Congregational Church, which had merged with the Christian Church and formed the United Church of Christ, which may one day be merging with the Methodist Church and the United Presbyterian Church, and, perhaps, Emily, with your Episcopal Church."

"Then," declared the observer, clasping my

hand, "you will be in excellent company!"

With which we started our walk, and almost immediately Bertha came by, having found a friend in the person of a bright-eyed young woman of Unity who immediately offered to take my visitors on a tour of the grounds, if I had other things to do, and if it would be all right with me. It was very much all right with me. What is it Unity says? *God's wisdom ever guides my way, working His good through me by the power of the Spirit within!*

But, for the sake of research, I did have one question to ask Bertha: "What brought *you* into Unity, outside of the fact that the fullness of time had come?"

And the convert said, "I have often wondered just what it was and how it came about. It wasn't a need for healing, as it is with many people. Actually it was not really any special need. I think it was simply that the Jesus I loved as a child did not satisfy me when I became an adult. But the consciousness of the Christ, the demonstration of God's goodness through Jesus as explained in Unity became marvelously satisfying and provable in my life. Then when I went to Unity services I always found something in them of practical help. You know, I have the feeling that when I go to Unity I am going to church and not going to church. Do you know what I mean?"

"There are services," I agreed, "which are more like a group of friends getting together and talking about life."

"And the joy of living!" said Bertha.

All of which, as the episode came back to me, suggested the joy and the miracle of remembrance which in the coming and going stages of life give continuity to the order of things.

I am thinking now, as I do my packing, many of the same thoughts that possessed me then. There are always converts, seekers, and observers. There are those who feel that Unity is a religion of temporization, complying with conditions of life with a temporary faith and then mulling them over later on. Some consider it a religion with a finely tuned rationale, in which make-believe plays a role and imagination has a part. And I found myself saying, "If it be imagination, let us have more of it, and if it be the secret power of faith, let us have more faith."

There is room, it seems to me, for one religion that sets up faith flares along humanity's trouble road and keeps the traffic moving. There is room in the world for one religion that has not only a light touch but a deeply adventurous quality which says that things are in divine order when they appear not to be so to the outer eye; a religion which dares to affirm: *Thank You, Father, for this apparent reversal in my fortune, for it is not a reversal; it carries a message which will be revealed to me;* one religion that says, as I heard a Unity member say: *Thank God for my aching back! It gives me a chance to prove the divine power of healing.* And he might have added, "And it tells me I should get at the cause behind the symptoms"; one religion which understands that all religion is a quest—for *good.*

Since there are sufficient groups emphasizing original sin, let there be one that reminds us of original virtue. Because there is a preponderance of movements stressing the Lord's chastening power, let there be one that insists upon His wish to love and bless.

As our ever-accelerating world rushes toward a new century, there will be new religious prophets claiming infallible directives from the throne of God. Let there be one religion with doctrines as human as those found in the Sermon on the Mount and as challenging as the life of Him who lived them.

Among the cavalcades of faiths that pay

342

homage to tradition, let there be one that respects the constant unfoldment of Truth; one religion that is not interested in statistics or sensationalism, commercialism or clout. Let it rather be a fellowship of faith, impartial as to how its ideals are propagated, a modern movement justifying itself on what it has to give, not get, on what it had yet to learn as well as on what it has found, and on what it now is as well as what it may become.

Thoughts of this kind could have continued indefinitely but for the buzzing of the telephone on the bedside table. It seems that in one's coming and going there is always the dramatic interlude of a phone call. This one was from the Unity switchboard with two messages. I would be picked up at noon for the drive to the airport. A ministerial student had arranged with my hosts to chauffeur me to Kansas City and have a chat along the way. Second message: A young couple at the reception center wanted to see me for a moment. They had a book to be autographed and, if convenient, they would be right over. They were sure I would remember that we were together two years ago.

I did not remember their names, but when they came to the door it was almost a case of *déjà vu*, the feeling that I had gone through all this before: greeting them in the tiny hallway, taking their hands, commenting on the beauty of the day. It *had* happened before, during my previous stay.

They had visited with me then, just as they were doing now. Again they were seated on the divan near the window that overlooks the grounds. I was comfortable in the high-backed gothic chair across from them. All was a replay of the former scene.

This time they came to tell me that the problem they had discussed with me, and which I had written about in my "Questions on the Quest" correspondence, had been solved. It had to do with parental opposition to their intended marriage, a Catholic-Protestant equation. Taking the responsibility upon themselves, they were married a year-and-a-half earlier by a Unity minister and joined a Unity church while time and changes in attitude and thought reconciled both parents and all was well.

This would have amounted to little more than routine business but for the matter of the book they wanted autographed. I had suggested during our first meeting that they read *The Unity Way of Life*. They picked up a copy at the time and now showed me how they had underlined and highlighted passages which were especially meaningful to them. I turned the pages, reassured that the book had been used not only for reading but for living.

Expressing my appreciation, I said, "How would you like this autographed, as of now or as of our first get-together?"

"We wondered," said the girl, "if you would mind autographing it to our baby?"

"Very good!" I agreed. "What is your baby's name?"

"We don't know as yet," the young man spoke up.

I was caught in the sudden, obvious realization of the subtle art of designers of maternity wear.

"Well, congratulations!" I said, "And thanks for the disclosure. When is the birthday?"

"Three months," said he.

"More or less," said she. "Write in it whatever you like, whatever you want. We thought it would be nice."

I took the book to the desk at the end of the room, got my green pen in hand, and found myself writing, "To a Child of God—Welcome to Planet Earth and Unity."

They liked that, and so did I.

The beauty of this incident stayed with me

long after we joined hands in a word of prayer and reminded ourselves that "no parting in Spirit" is the best possible way of saying good-bye.

I dare say that every visitor to Unity Village brings something in the way of spiritual meaning, and receives something in return. Giving and getting are like the lanes that wind into the Village from the highway—they run both ways.

Noon came after other telephone calls and other farewells, and I was on the way to the airport with my driver escort, Riley Allen, in his compact car. For some reason, when I was told that a student would pick me up, I had somehow expected a just-out-of-college ministerial candidate. This is what comes of traditionally orthodox assumptions. My chauffeur was young of heart but mature to a point of early middle age. He was one of the many seminarians who have been successful in professional careers. In his case, it was the military.

The military. He had every inch the qualities of a military man according to my stereotyped concept. He was athletically built, confident, straight-forward, and alert of mind. Had he been in uniform, there would have been no question about his rank of lieutenant colonel, which was his status when the call to the ministry came to him. He was in his final year of ministerial studies. His goal was to be ordained and get a center placement. (But he was destined to be named director of Unity School's Promotion department.)

For the first few miles his ministerial work was the gist of our conversation. From Charles and Myrtle Fillmore on to today, the challenges, effectiveness, societal involvements, and the demands of the "job" were subjects of interest. Not only "on to today," but on to the Unity of tomorrow, to the upcoming decades, to the vision of the 21st century and Unity's role in the world.

The ministry and the world. This was where I realized again the uncanny order of things as they happen to me, for nothing could have been more informative than to exchange views with this man who had gone straight to ministerial school from the military.

Here was a challenge not only to Unity but to every religious discipline, and a challenge to me as a professed researcher, to grasp somehow the immensity of a seemingly insurmountable, constantly increasing problem of war and peace.

347

A personal religion is one thing, a global religion another. Or are they different? Can they be different?

Allen had taken an oath to defend and serve his country. He would also be bound by an oath of conscience when he accepted his ordination to serve God. Are the two commitments compatible? Legally, in America, he could use his ministerial status as a valid reason for not engaging in armed conflict. As for defending one's country against armed aggression, that is countenanced by most religions and Scripture. It was not conscience we were talking about as much as *consciousness*.

In a world where the line of demarcation between building for defense and building for aggressive action is finer than a razor's edge, the matter of consciousness plays a part beyond human contemplation. We were asking ourselves whether the United States and the world were creating a war in *mind* to such a degree that we are drawing the actuality of war into existence.

These were the central thoughts in his mind and mine: The direction of consciousness in military power and God power; the equation of military might and the need for a mighty faith; nuclear reality and the reality of miracles of mind greater than the miracles of MX missiles in Minuteman silos dotting the land.

Unity, a personal adventure, taking a look at Unity on a global scale. We considered the equation of generations of ABMs (Anti-Ballistic Missiles) with their capability to kill versus new generations of human beings with their wish to live; the vulnerability of America's ABMs via the vulnerability of Soviet ABMs; the quality of what is now referred to as the relative power of the "first strike," the balance of power in warhead superiority, the rate of efficiency in activating the bombers in the air, the submarines in the seas, the tanks and artillery on the ground; nuclear planning and spiritual planning . . . I had to pinch myself back to reality to think that even the very talk of all this took place while traveling a friendly freeway in a free and friendly land. It was understandable only on the basis of the fact that my driver was a man familiar with both worlds, the world of faith in power and the world of the power of faith.

I thought about Allen a great deal after we clasped hands and blessed each other and parted at the air terminal. He was bound to bring some new thinking into his work, as are all ministerial candidates who come into Unity from "secular" careers. They should be expected to help put religion into a perspective far beyond the isolated concept of seclusion from the world, as was my destiny in my early ministerial training.

Yet, by divine order and the nature of my work, I have seen religions born, have watched them grow, have seen some die. Most of all, I have followed them as they took their places in the national and international context of our nation's life, and I have also seen them level out into "just another denomination."

Far be it from me to predict Unity's destiny or prophesy its future. That is up to Unity. What I do know beyond the shadow of a doubt and what I will predict is that there will always be a faith like the Unity I have described, for there is something in the human heart that wants and needs what Unity School of Christianity has to give.

And what is that?

A God of peace, a Son of love, a Spirit of joy.

As I flew to California through the pleasant skies of the nation that is home to me, I thought deeply about the inscription I put into the book for the young couple and their

350

soon-to-be firstborn, "To a Child of God—Welcome to Planet Earth and Unity."

I wished just now that I had added one more line, "Make it an adventure!"

But I didn't, and we will let it stand, knowing, as we all do in our coming and going, that divine order is ever in control.

The Unity Way . . . .